IMAGES OF ENGLAND

Bermondsey &
Rotherhithe
remembered

Bermondsey & Rotherhithe
remembered

Stephen Humphrey

Frontispiece: Sailing barges near the Angel from 1914 to 1915.

First published in 2004 by Tempus Publishing
Reprinted 2006,

Reprinted in 2008 by
The History Press
The Mill, Brimscombe Port,
Stroud, Gloucestershire, GL5 2QG
www.thehistorypress.co.uk

Reprinted 2009

British Library Cataloguing in Publication Data.
A catalogue record for this book is available from the British Library.

ISBN 978 0 7524 3316 5

Typesetting and origination by Tempus Publishing Limited.
Printed and bound in England.

Contents

Acknowledgements

I am indebted to many individuals for help in the compilation of this book. Above all, I am grateful to the contributors of reminiscences, whose writings make up the backbone of this book: Mr Peter Goode, who has also provided useful information on subjects beyond his own; Miss Barbara Stamford-Plows; Mr Fred Hill; Mr John Caley, who has also taken the trouble to attend my talks at the Blue Anchor Library over many years; Mr and Mrs Fred Newman; Mrs Joan Newstead; Mrs B.V. Roffe; and Mr John Beasley, a pillar of local history in the London Borough of Southwark who is unfailingly generous with historical information. I am grateful, too, to Mrs Ruth Mills for kindly giving me permission to publish substantial passages from the memoirs of her late father, Cyril Bustin. I fondly remember his coming to see me regularly in the 1980s, when he was writing them, and when he told me many of the stories which fortunately he wrote down in his inimitable style.

Fred Hill's reminiscences first appeared in the *Redcliffe Chronicle*, the magazine of the Rotherhithe and Bermondsey Local History Group. I gladly thank its former Editor, Stuart Rankin, for permission to use passages from those reminiscences, and also thank both him and Andrew Cockerill for kindly allowing me to publish the photograph of the participants at the first symposium on shipbuilsing on the Thames, which was held at Rotherhithe in the autumn of 2000. The illustrations are otherwise reproduced by kind permission of Ruth Jenkins, Local Studies Lbrarian at Southwark Local Studies Library. Without them, the book would be a great deal less lively and appealing.

Two further debts must be mentioned. One past correspondent, Mr Raymond Bates, was generous in giving me details of his research on the local 'purchase' of Flying Fortresses in the Second World War, which I acknowledge with many thanks. The local history of any district is made up from the specialist contributions of many hands. Finally I refer to the correspondence I have had over the last year with a local historian in Volgograd, the former Stalingrad, as a result of which I was prompted to look into the wartime connections between Bermondsey and the Soviet Union. I had been aware of a leaflet which showed Churchill and Stalin on the front, but I knew nothing of all the other details I have now unearthed.

Introduction

More than twenty years ago, I began a talk in Bermondsey by showing a slide of the coat of arms belonging to Bermondsey Borough Council until 1965. To my surprise, a considerable wave of emotion and pleasure swept through the hall, because local people have long been proud of Bermondsey and Rotherhithe and have identified with their past unusually closely. Undoubtedly these areas may claim a proud history with significant contributions to London and to the country as a whole.

Until well after the Second World War, Bermondsey and Rotherhithe were among the foremost industrial areas of England. Their commercial history is a roll-call not just of famous firms, but also of inventions. The first tinned food in the country was processed at Donkin's in Southwark Park Road, whose proprietor Bryan Donkin also invented the first practical printing machine and the first steel pen nib. The first corrugated iron was made nearby in Grange Road. The original Courage's Brewery was set up in Horselydown by the site of Tower Bridge in 1787. Peek Frean's made their first biscuits – the first familiar, modern soft biscuits – on the other side of St Saviour's Dock in the mid-nineteenth century. Benjamin Edgington's near London Bridge made equipment for some of the best-known nineteenth-century expeditions in Africa.

The local leather trade was likewise prominent. Tanneries abounded. A glance at the second edition of the 25" or 60" Ordnance survey sheets of 1894–96, on which surface water was coloured blue, at once reveals the myriad of open-air tanpits of the district. One firm, Barrow, Hepburn & Gale, contributed so many leather goods to the war effort in the 1940s that Field-Marshal Montgomery himself went to visit the firm's Grange Mills. C.W. Martin & Sons of the Alaska Factory nearby produced 345,000 processed sheepskins for use in the RAF's flying suits, and James Garnar & Sons manufactured 35 million sq ft of jerkin leather for the war effort, despite losing most of their Bermondsey buildings in the Blitz. Waste from tanneries went into other businesses. Some went to the hat-makers to make felt hats. The firm of Christy's in Bermondsey Street made beefeaters' hats and Churchill's homburgs (amidst much workaday headgear). Further waste went to make gelatine. 'Spa Gelatine', an edible grade made by B. Young & Co. Ltd in Grange Road, was used by Crosse & Blackwell just down the road (among a huge number of customers). Finally, bones went for glue-making and various allied trades. One enterprising individual, Charles Cordrey of Long Lane, was described in directories as 'ox feet and trotter dresser, genuine neat's foot and trotter oils, hoof and trotter manures, and dealer in ox bones and hoofs'. Nothing was wasted! The expression, 'Where there's muck there's brass', was clearly as applicable to Bermondsey as much as it was to the North of England.

Bermondsey was also at the forefront in the history of transport. The London and Greenwich Railway, opened in 1836, was London's first railway; and Spa Road Station

in the middle of Bermondsey had the honour of being London's first, albeit temporary, terminus. In the same era, Sir Marc Brunel and his son, Isambard Kingdom Brunel, were building the Thames Tunnel at Rotherhithe; it was the world's first underwater tunnel. The famous China tea clippers sailed to Hay's Wharf a generation later. The *Flying Spur* was built for Jardine, Matheson & Co. whose Far Eastern trade was closely allied with that of Hay's Wharf, itself the linchpin of 'London's larder'.

Rotherhithe was once a quite separate district under its own local government but became part of the Borough of Bermondsey in the twentieth century. Its commercial character was moulded by ships and the sea. Shipbuilding, ship-repairing and ship-breaking were its old staples and many firms built and repaired barges or lighters, the workhorses of the River Thames. The last barge-repairer, Charles Hay & Son, ceased to trade as recently as Christmas 1997. The Greenland Dock, first opened more than 300 years ago, became in the early nineteenth century part of a complex of docks which developed a leading role in the timber trade. By the twentieth century, there were nine wet docks, six timber ponds and a canal running 3.5 miles to Camberwell and Peckham.

Bermondsey's industrial strength might make one think that its people were prosperous but before the Second World War most of its population were relatively poor; wages were generally low and some lines of work were casual rather than regular. One old man reminiscing in recent years wrote that at Galleywall Road School, he had sung what were once called 'national songs', including *Rule Britannia,* with its line, 'Britons never shall be slaves'; when he went to work in local industry, with its long hours, low wages and hard routines, he had second thoughts about Britons never being slaves!

Pre-war poverty is reflected in countless pictures of narrow backstreets of terraced houses of which many examples are included in this book. These houses had no front gardens.

Above: Courage's brewery is seen here in 1963 from Horselydown Lane. By that date, Courage's had merged with Barclay, Perkins & Co. Ltd; its Southwark rival a little upstream.

Opposite: The heart of Bermondsey in 1926. The main road on the left is Southwark Park Road (bottom) and Grange Road (top), with Dunton Road joining on the bend. Rouel Road cuts off to the right, past the old Lipton's factory, in the foreground, which had previously been a jam factory and even earlier a tannery. Towards the top right, next to the railway, are the Neckinger Leather Mills of Bevingtons & Sons. The road running past them is Neckinger, heading diagonally towards Spa Road. In that street one can see the white-fronted town hall, which was bombed in the Second World War and, to the left of it, the Bermondsey central library. To the south of Spa Road are Atkinson's, Young's and Pearce Duff's, all major factories. The empty site next to the town hall was used to build the municipal offices which became the town hall after the bombing. At the top, to the left, is the Alaska Factory of C.W. Martin & Sons Ltd, and in the centre, the Grange Mills belonging to Barrow, Hepburn & Gale. The empty space to the left of centre – a playground – had been the site of Donkin's the engineers. The streets at bottom left formed parts of the West Estate.

Courage's brewery by Tower Bridge in 1976. Riverside breweries were once numerous. This was the site of the firm's original brewery, founded in 1787. Courage's vacated this site in 1982 and so ended nearly two centuries of occupation. The buildings seen here have been preserved. Note Horselydown Old Stairs emerging from under the right-hand end of the brewery, one of the ancient river stairs so characteristic of the waterfront of Bermondsey and Rotherhithe.

Crosse & Blackwell (in the background on the right), the Alaska Factory belonging to C.W. Martin & Sons Ltd (with the chimney) and the Grange Road baths (with the clock) in 1956. This photograph was taken from the roof of the central library in Spa Road. This vicinity had long been devoted to industry. Many tanneries were sited in the Grange area just to the right, including the very substantial firm of Barrow, Hepburn & Gale. On the left, near the junction of Spa Road and Grange Road, the first corrugated iron was manufactured in England.

Hay's Wharf, *c.* 1938. A typical scene of the working river, made up of ships, cranes and warehouses. All this was normal until about 1970 all along the Bermondsey and Rotherhithe waterfront.

Their doors opened directly into the living-rooms as a rule. There were rarely any back gardens either; just a yard in most cases. Architectural decoration was absent unless the houses were survivors of better days as in certain streets in Horselydown or in Princes Street at Rotherhithe. The doorframes of such houses were sometimes notable. Otherwise the most that backstreet pre-war houses could show were ground-floor window shutters which were always pinned back. The landlords were absentees, needless to say. One landlord could own a substantial area – several streets with factories, shops and even chapels included – and the landlord's forebears had often acquired the land when it consisted of fields. Each property would be leased out and sometimes sub-leased with the actual occupiers or tenants well down the ladder. In the poorest properties near the river, there was constant coming and going, at least in the nineteenth century. Work was casual on the riverfront and so was the housing.

The transformation of Bermondsey began in the 1920s at the hands of the borough council and of the London County Council. Many blocks of flats were built between the wars. In 1939, however, the greater part of the old borough still stood; it was the Second World War that brought a far greater change. For one thing, the population fell drastically. The borough of Bermondsey had 111,542 people in 1931 but only 60,640 in 1951. Many of those who served in the armed forces or who were evacuated never returned to Bermondsey. Some of the reminiscences in this book tell of the writers' families remaining elsewhere after 1945. Bermondsey's post-war Member of Parliament, Robert

The Surrey Docks, looking west, in 1926. The timber sheds and the timber ponds can clearly be seen in this view and also the long line of riverside sides round the peninsula, broken in the foreground by Nelson Dock where ships were repaired until the 1960s.

Mellish, was one of those who stayed elsewhere, in a suburb further out. Much property was destroyed in the war and so in the two decades after 1945 considerable rebuilding took place. Employment was buoyant in those years and pay much higher than it had been before 1939. A more prosperous era arrived but in an attenuated and looser community. Then came the exodus of industry, especially in the 1960s and 1970s, and the gradual redevelopment of the industrial areas, largely for housing. The face of Bermondsey, above all near the riverfront, changed drastically.

It will be readily observed that the pre-war backstreets were almost entirely devoid of traffic. As a result they formed the playgrounds of the young until 1939. There were very few open spaces and the only one of any size was Southwark Park.

The metropolitan borough of Bermondsey existed from 1900 to 1965. Previously, there were five civil parishes: St Mary Magdalen's, Bermondsey; St Mary's, Rotherhithe; St Olave's, Southwark; St. John's, Southwark (or St John's, Horselydown); and St Thomas's, Southwark. The parishes of Bermondsey and Rotherhithe both built a town hall in the late nineteenth century but after 1900 only the one in Spa Road retained the role. Spa Road became Bermondsey's civic centre. In 1965 the borough was merged with its neighbours, Southwark and Camberwell, but it is certainly not forgotten. Former Bermondsey folk and their descendants keep up a world-wide interest.

Riverside Wharves: London's Larder

The western end of Tooley Street, 1967, before the building of Colechurch House on the site in the foreground. In succeeding years, Toppings Wharf and its neighbours to the left were demolished. The square-cut building slightly to the right was the head office of the Proprietors of Hay's Wharf who owned practically all the property between London Bridge and Tower Bridge. Cargo-handling was predominant in this quarter, especially the handling of foodstuffs. Tooley Street was known as 'London's larder'. The wharf building, with its tiers of openings or 'loopholes' for cargoes, was the characteristic building of Tooley Street and of virtually the entire riverfront of the borough. The closure of the upstream docks from the late 1960s onwards made most of the wharves redundant.

Hay's Wharf traced its origins to the mid-seventeenth century. The last proprietor who belonged to the founding family was Francis Theodore Hay who owned the business until 1838. The partnership which succeeded him was dominated by John Humphery who served as Alderman and Lord Mayor of London. In his time, alliances with traders in the Far East brought the China tea trade to Tooley Street. The clipper ships or fast sailing ships of the mid-nineteenth century would race from Foochow to Hay's Wharf for example, with the new season's tea. A painting which is often reproduced shows the *Flying Spur* arriving at Hay's Dock on the Southwark waterfront in 1862 at the end of that year's race. Tea remained an important part of the Hay's Wharf business until the twentieth century, as the pictures below show. A public house called the Horniman at Hay's was opened in the 1980s in the restored warehouses to recall the old tea trade.

Hay's Dock, *c.* 1920. The wet dock was filled in and the warehouses were converted into offices and shops in the late 1980s under the title of Hay's Galleria. In this view, tea is being unloaded from the barges into the warehouses. The introduction of refrigerated ships brought the dairy trade to Hay's Wharf, especially from Australia and New Zealand. In the twentieth century, there was even an office of New Zealand's Department of Agriculture in Tooley Street. The London Provision Exchange was also housed nearby.

Tea being bulked at Hay's Wharf, *c.* 1920.

Tea being repacked for export in Hay's Wharf, *c.* 1920.

Mark Browne's Wharf, c. 1958. Individual warehouses in the Hay's Wharf had distinctive names, which were generally those that applied before they became part of the group.

Food Processing

Working at Crosse & Blackwell between 1948 and the closure of the factory in 1969
By Peter Goode

I started work in the laboratories of the Crosse & Blackwell factory following my 'demob' from National Service in 1948. At first, whilst living at home, I rose at an ungodly hour to travel by Southern Railway to Waterloo and then took a No.1 bus. This brought me to the stop opposite the old Bermondsey baths in Grange Road a couple of minutes' walk from the factory in Crimscott Street. I soon got tired of this so obtained 'digs' in Stockwell from where I travelled to Bermondsey by tube to the Elephant and then by tram.

The Crosse & Blackwell factory was located in Crimscott Street at the end of which was Willow Walk with Hearson's laboratory equipment works and beyond that the extensive railway yards, formerly part of Bricklayer's Arms' station. At the rear of the factory and of the adjacent Alaska Works was Curtis Street, named after the botanist William Curtis who had established an early botanical nursery gardens in the area around the end of the eighteenth century.

The premises of Crosse & Blackwell in Crimscott Street, *c.* 1930.

On the north side of C'St was the canteen, the yard where barrels of brined vegetables were kept and the staff shop. I recall a very early visit to this shop and proudly taking home cans of luncheon meat to mother; they had cost me the princely sum of one (old) penny each! Also on a personal note: the factory had a social club and besides playing tennis, in the early 1950s I became involved with the Amateur Dramatic Group which put on performances at the Rotherhithe assembly hall.

The building in which the laboratories were located had once been the factory of the Elisabeth Lazenby company and dated from around 1897. Crosse & Blackwell arrived following a merger and greatly expanded operations on the site, putting up major new buildings in 1924 and again in 1927.

Among the products manufactured at C'St (as Crimscott Street was always known in the company) was a large range of canned goods – including soups, luncheon meat, baked beans, peas and spaghetti. The glass packed lines included salad cream, tomato ketchup, Branston pickle and sauce, meat and fish pastes, essences and flavourings. The company also had associated factories at Silvertown, Peterhead and Dundee.

At first I was principally involved with routine microbiological quality control work. One of the functions of the laboratories was the handling of consumer complaints which, with the very best will in the world, any manufacturer will inevitably receive. Although these constituted only a very small proportion of the total production, they were always taken very seriously; their investigation and the steps needed to prevent their recurrence became a part of my work. I also had occasion from time to time to visit various riverside wharves to collect samples of imported ingredients, such as tomato puree for ketchup and sultanas which went into Branston pickle. Likewise, I would visit the vinegar brewery in Tower Bridge Road, itself a part of the Crosse & Blackwell group.

Day-to-day work aside, in around 1950 I was asked to open up some tea chests found in the loft of our building and in which some thoughtful person had, before the war, 'put-down' a representative collection of products being manufactured there in the 1930s. With some guidance from the Victoria & Albert Museum, I got these into museum condition and for many years we had them on display in our foyer.

I later became increasingly involved with other administrative work and with the setting up of a small technical library. I recall our having both an early (and gigantic)

An aerial view, showing Crosse & Blackwell's premises, *c.* 1938. The factory is in the middle in Crimscott Street. Grange Road is running diagonally upwards from the left, and its junction with Spa Road may be seen at the top. Willow Walk runs across the picture below it.

The main entrance to B. Young & Co. Ltd's works at 123 Grange Road in 1964. The firm was listed in directories as 'manufacturers of edible, pharmaceutical, photographic and technical gelatines'.

Xerox copier and a primitive word processor which worked on the same principle as a pianola piano player – long before computers came into use! As Librarian, and subsequently an Information Officer, I had occasion to make frequent use of the very valuable service of the then Bermondsey borough library in Spa Road.

In the same building we also had a laboratory concerned with the development of new processes and products together with an analytical laboratory. Over the years these functions were greatly expanded adding a home economics kitchen, a pilot plant and workshops for the construction of experimental equipment, eventually spawning a semi-autonomous development unit.

From 1958 onwards I walked daily to the Crosse & Blackwell factory from London Bridge Station. The route via St Thomas' Street and Bermondsey Street with its numerous side alleys became quite familiar to me. On some Friday mornings, I would try to be early enough to spend a few minutes perusing the stalls of the Caledonian market in Bermondsey Square. Just beyond this square was the old Trocette Cinema – an offshoot, presumably, of the very grand Trocadero at the Elephant.

In Grange Road there was the large and odorous Barrow, Hepburn & Gale leather factory. Also in Grange Road was Molin's who manufactured cigarette-making machines; the Alaska seal fur factory and the Heinke company which produced diving equipment were also on this road.

In the Spa Road and Alscot Road area I recall Young's gelatine factory partly because it was so notorious for its smells and partly because their Spa Gelatine was used in the manufacture of Crosse & Blackwell's calves' foot jelly.

In 1964 the company became the subject of a take-over battle, being acquired by the Nestlé group and not surprisingly this eventually resulted in rationalisation of production over fewer sites. I was at this time on the staff of the development unit, which under Nestlé was their *de facto* London research company and became known as Londreco. We were the last to leave Crimscott Street, moving to the Nestlé site at Hayes in Middlesex late in 1969.

The site as a whole has since become an industrial complex housing a wide variety of separate businesses. The original Lazenby building still stands and in 2004 is being used by the Law Society as a document store.

The archives of Crosse & Blackwell have recently been deposited with the London Metropolitan Archives, and the museum pieces referred to are now located in the Alimentarium, the Nestlé museum in Vevey in Switzerland.

B. Young & Co. Ltd

B. Young & Co. Ltd produced various grades of gelatine in premises situated between Grange Road and Spa Road. The firm made use of tannery waste in its processes and the works gave off a strong aroma, but a twentieth-century booklet advertising the firm was nevertheless entitled *The Romance of Bermondsey*. Gelatine was produced for industrial and photographic purposes but Spa Gelatine was a well-known edible grade used, for example, by Crosse & Blackwell in their nearby factory. A neighbour of Young's was Atkinson's Eonia Works of 1910, which was a perfumery (later Unilever's central perfumery). Young's was so anxious about industrial espionage that it used codes to explain its processes for its own internal purposes.

Lipton's and Pearce Duff's
By Fred Hill

Situated halfway down Rouel Road was Lipton's factory where much of their grocery products were manufactured or prepared. In the 1930s Lipton's was a very important firm. Every market place or High Street worthy of the name had its Lipton's shop. The entrance to the Lipton's building in Rouel Road faced a very large church hall. I don't know anything about it but I believe it was one of the Free Churches.

We move up Rouel Road to its junction with Spa Road. Established in a private house in 1847, Pearce Duff & Co. eventually moved here. I became their office boy in 1932; my technical training went by the board as a job was the thing. Pearce Duff's buildings merit a comment and give an indication of the manner of their growth. The offices were sited at the junction of Rouel and Spa Roads and were formerly a pub. The walls of the whole of the ground floor were covered in deep green tiles and although the building was demolished many years ago, traces could still be seen on the undeveloped site until recently. Pearce Duff was one of the country's largest manufacturers and processors of custard powder, baking powder, culinary flavourings, essences and colourings. They strove to be self-sufficient not only in the manufacture of their products but also in colour printing and the manufacture of cardboard boxes, skillets, etc.

The Managing Director was Daniel Duff, an early middle-aged man, severe, beetle-browed and with the voice of a parade ground sergeant-major. He was very aware and knew everything that was going on.

Pearce Duff's premises in Spa Road in 1976 after the closure of the factory.

I have always remembered the example he set me. I had been with the company two or three days when the telephone rang; I answered it: 'Hello, Pearce Duff'. In due course, I replaced the receiver. Then from across the other side of the office came the commanding cry: 'Boy! Don't waste my time and my money. Don't say 'Hello', just say 'Pearce Duff'. 'Yessir', I said. His lips twitched and I scurried away. The other director was an elderly man named Cockshead. He must have hated his name because no one dared use it. He insisted upon being called 'Mr Cohead'.

The factory buildings were a leftover from the days when leather tanning was the main industry of Bermondsey. They had windows especially designed to allow the maximum movement of air. These windows were about 3ft long and about 9ins in width with central swivels which allowed over ninety degrees of rotation. There is an amusing story which features these particular type windows. When powder products such as custard and blancmange were being manufactured, traces would float in the air and find their way to the open windows where they would settle. If a window was disturbed, the deposit would fall to the ground beneath or, in this particular case, onto a passer-by! He was a city office manager and the powder fell onto his bowler hat and back of his raincoat, quite unnoticed by him. He was aware of people staring but did not think it was anything to do with him until he arrived at his office. Angry words with Pearce Duff followed, and then the apologies. This occurred before my time, so I cannot vouch for the truth of the story.

Another humorous characteristic of Pearce Duff was that all receipts for goods must be signed for by a clerk in the main office. Since the warehouseman with the receiving note could be 60 yards away, delays of over several minutes were inevitable; exasperated drivers would write on the wall with thick crayon, 'Died waiting' with the appropriate date and time.

A Bermondsey Childhood

By Barbara Stamford-Plows

Shuttleworth's chocolates

In 1956, I was working on a conveyor belt at Shuttleworth's chocolate factory in Galleywall Road. At the time I was at loggerheads with my father and refused to consider a 'whitecollar' job, which was the height of his ambition for me. The factory paid £4 a week so I felt quite rich. You could eat as much chocolate as you liked, but after the first week you weren't bothered unless something new came on line. I was mostly wrapping Christmas-tree decorations in tinfoil. They had a good staff canteen where you could get a decent meal at lunch time for 7d. I worked there until we moved to Brighton.

Bermondsey smells

Some of the things I remember most about living in Bermondsey are the smells. Apart from the all-pervading smell of the tanneries there was the smell of lavender from Yardley's, vinegar from the pickle factory, fruit from Hartley's, and the smell of baking from Peek Frean's. After Dunkirk my father was stationed at Woolwich for a while and 'moonlighted' at Hartley's jam factory. I don't know what went on there but my mother was not allowed to buy Hartley's jam! My mother worked at Peek Frean's for a while then she worked at Chillingworth's bakery shop next to the Baths and Farrell's café in Old Kent Road.

Neckinger Leather Mills in Abbey Street in 1976.

Leather Manufacture:
There's Nothing Like Leather

Bevingtons & Sons

The biggest firm of leather manufacturers in Bermondsey was Bevingtons & Sons whose works in Abbey Street were known as Neckinger Leather Mills. One large building still stands just north of the railway viaduct and south of Old Jamaica Road. The firm took over the site from a paper manufacturer in the early 1800s and traded there until the 1980s. The London & Greenwich railway was built across the site in 1833–36 but production continued in the two halves and also under the arches. The firm was chiefly engaged in the light leather trade: morocco leather, roans (sheepskins tanned in sumac, a substance brought from Sicily), skivers (the grain side of sheepskins split before tanning), sealskins, cape hat linings, and chamois leathers.

In the late nineteenth and early twentieth centuries, the firm was headed by Samuel Bourne Bevington (1832–1907) who was one of the most notable industrial and civic leaders of Bermondsey. He served as the first Mayor of the metropolitan borough of Bermondsey in 1900–02; he commanded the 3rd Volunteer Battalion of the Royal West Surrey Regiment (later the 22nd London Regiment) and built their drill hall next to his works at the corner of Old Jamaica Road; he also held all manner of local public offices. A statue of him was erected in Tooley Street in 1911.

In the twentieth century the tannery became more and more the province of the chemist and the laboratory technician, and of machinery. The southern half of Neckinger Mills was sold to Bermondsey Borough Council for housing in the 1930s but the rest remained in industrial use for another fifty years.

The finishing shop of Neckinger Leather Mills in June 1931.

Top: The mantelpiece at 148 Long Lane, *c.* 1920. A ground–floor room of the house contains this interesting memento of the local leather industry. The property was renovated in the 1970s. The same street boasts the Simon the Tanner public house.

Above: The doorway of the Leather Exchange in Weston Street in 1979. Carved roundels depicting processes in leather manufacture are placed above the windows. The Exchange was built curiously at a time when leather tanning in Bermondsey was contracting. The Rouel Road tannery became a jam factory at the end of the century, for example, and the Guinness Buildings in Page's Walk were also built on the site of a tannery.

Following pages: Glazing snakeskins in the Neckinger Leather Mills in 1931.

Engineering

Donkin's

Bryan Donkin (1768-1855) was the founder of one of Bermondsey's most significant businesses, which had premises in Southwark Park Road from 1803 to 1902. He was a notable inventor and pioneer. He built the first practical paper-making machine, he invented the steel pen nib and he was the pioneer in England in canning food.

He was originally summoned to Bermondsey by Henry and Sealy Foundrinier as an expert in paper-making machinery and by 1807 he had perfected a sound, practical machine.

As for food canning, the inventor was Nicholas Appert of Paris. Donkin was the pioneer in England. His early tins were decidedly heavy and the instructions for opening them even recommended the use of a hammer and chisel. Sample tins of beef were sent in 1813 to the Duke of Kent (son of King George III and father of Queen Victoria) from whose secretary came remarkable praise: 'It was tasted by the Queen, the Prince Regent, and several distinguished personages and highly approved'. He fared less well with the Duke of Wellington's household. An aide of the Duke's brother (Marquess Wellesley) replied that Lord Wellesley could not reply himself as he was 'so much indisposed'. He nevertheless complimented the firm on its tinned food and encouraged the sending of tins for military and naval trials under the Duke's patronage.

Tinned meat to the value of £3,000 was sold by the firm in the first half of 1817; this was a stupendous sum for the times.

In the mid-nineteenth century, Bryan Donkin produced a gas valve which proved to be in great demand by a burgeoning industry. Donkin's became a firm of gas engineers. By the end of the Victorian era, the firm considered it needed to be nearer the coal and steel industries and removed in 1902 to Chesterfield in Derbyshire.

Above: The unveiling of the plaque on 17 October 1960 by Harold Shearman, the chairman of the London County Council's education committee.

Opposite: The plaque in Southwark Park Road commemorating Donkin & Gamble's canning factory.

Dewrance's at Great Dover Street in the 1930s.

Dewrance's

Dewrance & Co. Ltd, engineers in Great Dover Street, had a connection with
Stephenson's *Rocket*. There was a painting of the *Rocket* in the main hall. The products
of Dewrance's were world-renowned and could be repaired after years of good service.
Some of their smaller valves were in use in the Bank of England and when in 1969 I
mentioned the fact to one of their engineers, having seen the valves working, he said, 'We
all wish that these valves were still being manufactured'.

Fred Newman

Sir John Dewrance (1858-1937)

Born in Peckham, he was the only son of John Dewrance who had erected the
locomotive, *Rocket*, for George Stephenson. John Dewrance was educated at Charterhouse
and King's College in London, where he paid special attention to chemistry. On coming
of age, he took control of the engineering business of Dewrance & Co., which had been
left to him by his father. He started a research laboratory in which he produced an ingot
of aluminium by electrolysis in 1882. John Dewrance was a prolific inventor who took
out more than a hundred patents, mainly relating to steam fittings and boiler mountings.
From 1899 until shortly before his death, he was chairman of Babcock and Wilcox Ltd.
In 1923 he was president of the Institution of Mechanical Engineers. He was appointed
KBE in 1920 and GBE in 1928. His publications included *The Corrosion of Marine Boilers*
and *Machinery Bearings*.

John Beasley

Docks and Wharves at Rotherhithe

Top: The riverfront at King's Stairs in 1911. This was one of the ancient watermen's stairs, recalling in their name the nearby site of King Edward III's fourteenth-century mansion. Often, watermen's stairs were associated with pubs and here they run underneath the Dover Castle, belonging to Hoare & Co. The property to the left of the stairs, originally No.41 Rotherhithe Street and now 1 Fulford Street, is the only survivor of this old waterfront apart from the Angel public house a little to the west. This property was for long occupied by Braithwaite & Dean, a firm of lightermen.

Above: The riverfront at the western end of Rotherhithe in 1953. Platform Wharf is on the right with the crane in front of it. Immediately behind the crane is the Angel public house, next to Rotherhithe Stairs. The tall chimney belonged to Gillman and Spencer at Gordon's Wharf. The steeple of St Mary in Rotherhithe may be seen farther left. John James designed the body of the church, which was built in 1714-15, and Lancelot Dowbiggin added the steeple in 1747-48. Note the great mass of lighters; many lighterage firms and barge repairers still operated in this district fifty years ago.

Greenland Dock in 1926. This was a generation after it had been extended and the lock greatly enlarged. Cunarders of 14,000 tons entered it in this era, plying to and from Canada. Canada Dock is shown at top left. Note the line of Redriff Road winding through the docks in the centre.

A Cunarder in the Surrey Docks.

Southwark Park with St Olave's Hospital below it and, at the bottom, Canada Dock with its timber yards in 1926. The Rotherhithe Hippodrome stands out in Lower Road. To the right is the pumping station in Renforth Street of the London Hydraulic Power Co. Until the Second World War, hydraulic power was still very important in the industrial parts of London. The works to the left of the chimney belonged to Brandram's, refiners of saltpetre and flowers of sulphur and manufacturers of white lead.

Nelson Dock House at Rotherhithe Street is one of the district's most historically resonant buildings. It dates from 1740 and reflects the prosperity which could come from Rotherhithe's maritime past. For much of its life, the house belonged to the shipbuilding and ship-repairing businesses which occupied the adjacent land. In particular, it belonged to the business run by Randall & Brent, and afterwards by the Brents on their own, in the later eighteenth and early nineteenth centuries.

Left: An engraving of Samuel Brent. This probably represents Samuel Brent Snr, who died in 1814. The Brent family built many ships for the Royal Navy during the various French wars, and also ships for the East India Co. There were additionally some pioneering vessels. Daniel Brent built the *Rising Star* in 1821, which was one of the first steam warships and the first steamship to cross the Atlantic under power. It was built for Lord Cochrane, the British admiral who helped the Chileans gain their independence from Spain in the early nineteenth century.

A Bank of England cheque for £10,100, made payable to Samuel Brent Jnr in March 1815, three months before the Battle of Waterloo. This was a stupendous sum at that time, and must represent a share in the firm's capital after the elder Samuel's death or upon the sale of the dockyard.

Nos 41-55 Rotherhithe Street in 1960. The Angel public house may be seen at the extreme left. These small riverfront properties had long been occupied by barge-builders and barge-repairers and, in earlier days, by mast-makers and sail-makers. Until the 1930s, the street here was very narrow and, in conjunction with numerous neighbouring streets, formed the densely-packed, historic heart of Rotherhithe. After the Second World War, unfortunately, the London County Council determined to replace this ancient vitality with parkland. There was a battle in the early 1960s to save these houses in which Sir John Betjeman took part. Only No.41, the tall house behind the street lamp on the left, was saved. The street itself was later swept away. It is unbelievable that the busy and ancient heart of Rotherhithe should have been treated so destructively.

Opposite below: Shipbuilding remembered in 2000. Stuart Rankin (seated), the historian of shipbuilding at Rotherhithe, arranged a symposium on the subject at Nelson Dock House in September 2000. This photograph of those attending was taken on the steps of the house. They included Bryan Cumings (top right) who was a former apprentice at Nelson Dock from 1948-53 and, immediately below him, Captain Brent Streit of the US Navy who was descended from Samuel Brent Junior (1787-1835), who migrated to the USA in 1829.

Lower Road in Rotherhithe, *c.* 1920.

A Bermondsey Milkman in 1970

By John Beasley

A scar on one of my fingers is a permanent reminder that over thirty years ago I was a milkman in Bermondsey and Rotherhithe.

As part of my round, I delivered one pint of milk every day to the park keeper's house in Southwark Park. As the garden had a low gate I used to jump over it but one day I tripped. The bottle broke and the glass cut my finger so badly that I went to a chemist's in Lower Road to ask the pharmacist to stop it bleeding.

When I was changing jobs in 1970, I had five weeks to spare so I became a milkman employed by the Royal Arsenal Co-operative Society. I had to get up at 4.15 a.m. and then drive a milk float from the depot in Camberwell Grove, where I then lived, to Bermondsey. One of my earliest calls was to Maydew House, a very tall block overlooking Southwark Park. As I had to deliver six crates of milk on a trolley, I used one of the two lifts but there were problems when one was broken and another milkman arrived at the same time as I did.

One day when I had parked next to another block of flats, I had to reverse the milk float so I looked out of the back window. As I saw no vehicles behind, I moved backwards but then heard a loud bang. I got out and discovered that I had hit a mini. The milk float was piled three crates high but the mini was as high as only a crate and a half so I did not see it. A very upset lady came out of the block of flats and asked: 'What shall I tell my husband?'

The only funny note I received requested 'an extra two cows today please'. I think the customer would have been very surprised if I had left two mooing cows on her doorstep.

Milk was 11½-d in 1970 as I sometimes remind one of my former customers, Rene Talbot, when I see her at Manor Methodist church where she has been a stalwart member for many years.

Two years after being a milkman in Bermondsey and Rotherhithe, I became a student social worker there and was based at Lady Gomm House – but that's another story!

The main entrance of the Surrey Commercial Docks in Lower Road in 1963. The office with its clock-tower, just within this entrance, has been retained on the approach road to the present Surrey Quays' Shopping Centre. In the 1980s, the office became the local base of the London Docklands Development Corporation.

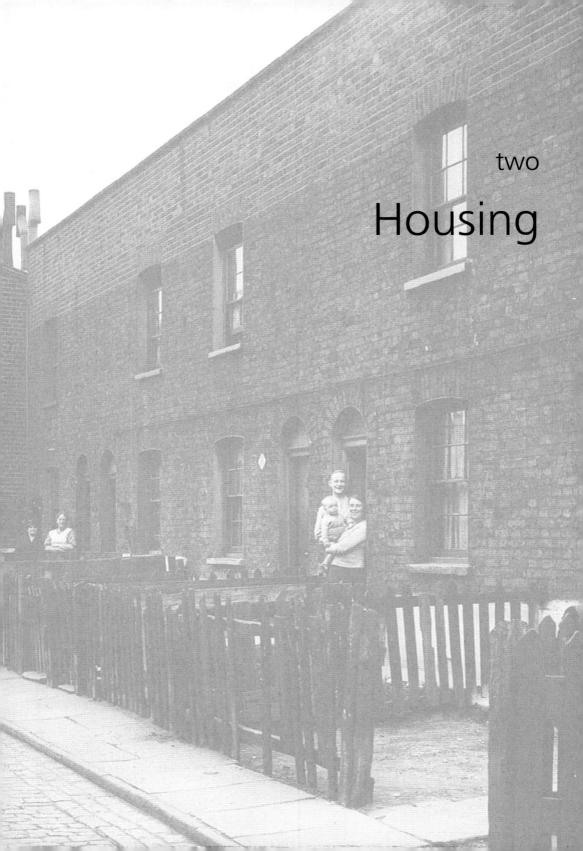

two

Housing

Reminiscences of Bermondsey

By Joan Newstead, née *Moore*

I was born in Larnaca Street in Bermondsey in 1925 when life was a far cry from modern times. Money was in short supply with most of the working class and all experienced hard times. As a small child I recall my father queuing to try to get work in the docks and coming home very dejected after failing to get employment. We had one bun in the house for food. Dad broke down and cried.

Dad managed to get work as a carman for a Mr Greenslade whose business was delivering vegetables etc. to the London restaurants and cafes. With the job was living accommodation in a flat over the stables at 44 Weston Street in Bermondsey. Part of Dad's job was to care for the six horses so my brother and I had a wonderful time playing in the stables.

I often spent great times out and about with Dad on his rounds. Living so near the station, we could hear from our bedroom the hop pickers getting their train at London Bridge to Kent early in the morning.

As children we played a lot in the street with whips and tops and tied ropes on the lamp posts to make a swing. Saturday afternoons was always a treat as all the mums, grandmas and aunties came out in the street to play Awlley-in-Together, a skipping game where as many people as you could find skipped together with one large rope. It was always great fun. Sunday afternoons we went for walks. A typical walk would be going from Weston Street over London Bridge, past the Monument, through Billingsgate, back over Tower Bridge and down Crucifix Lane to home.

In the corner shop Old Mother Brown would sell farthing dips. We would be so pleased to get a prize with more value than a farthing. I recall too the houses on Maze Pond where I played, now part of Guy's Hospital. I also remember the very old houses in Vinegar Yard close to London Bridge Station.

I recall the 'Blackshirts' of Sir Oswald Mosley causing quite a stir. We watched from our bedroom window the Blackshirts being chased down Weston Street. I remember my school in Long Lane having barriers across the road during this time.

On Saturday mornings, I would take my younger brother to the Tuppenny Rush at a local cinema. We would sit two to a seat to watch Buster Crabb films. In the interval a person would come round with a Flit gun which smelled of perfume. I think it was some form of fumigation.

In about 1934, Mother managed a bag wash shop. People would bring in their laundry in a white bag which was weighed then charged by weight. It was sent, I think, to the Sunlight Laundry.

My cousin had a grandfather who was Italian. He had an ice cream cart painted white with red, blue and gold emblems on it. The cart had two silver bowls on the top with lids. One bowl contained ice cream and the other iced water. In his Italian accent he would call out: 'Icer creamer'. He also had a bicycle with two front wheels and a box-shaped container from which he sold hot pies. He also sold chestnuts outside the cinemas. Since 1904 to this day, his brother's family have run the pie and mash shop in Tower Bridge Road called Manze's. We often went there as kids. The layout with the dummy waiter hasn't changed since I was a child. Just along the road to the pie and mash shop, Grandma Moore used to help out in the Medical Mission. She spent many hours there after being widowed, helping out as a volunteer.

Larnaca Street in 1929. This was a nineteenth-century residential street whose name, bestowed on it in 1880, was derived from the British acquisition of Cyprus in 1878.

Left: Tilbury Place in 1939. The original caption of this photograph reads: 'The last two inhabitants of Tilbury Place, Fair Street, just before demolition 1939'. Tilbury Place was a dead-end alley of about four houses which ran off Fair Street behind the present Devon mansions at the Tanner Street end. No doubt the houses were always modest and their occupants poor, but we can readily imagine how awful the two pictured here must have felt upon being forced out by municipal development. Slum clearance seemed essential to those who planned it but it must have seemed the end of the world to many of those it displaced.

Above: Lord Llangattock at The Hendre in Monmouthshire in 1903. John Allan Rolls, Lord Llangattock, was the owner of large parts of Bermondsey, Southwark and Camberwell. His family seems to have come from Monmouthshire originally but went to Bermondsey in the eighteenth century, initially with the lowly label of cowkeepers. In the late eighteenth century, John Rolls became a property developer and lived at the Grange, near the junction of Grange Road and Spa Road. He had made a fortune by his death in 1801. His son, another John Rolls, built a big mansion in the Old Kent Road at its junction with Dunton Road but lived there only briefly before migrating to the West End. It was his grandson, depicted here, who was given a peerage in 1892. The peer's younger son was Charles Stewart Rolls, the joint-founder of Rolls-Royce. Unfortunately, both he and his brother met violent ends and so the family estates were inherited by Lord Llangattock's daughter, Lady Shelley-Rolls, who lived until 1961. In this picture, Lord Llangattock is holding the loving cup to the left of the doorway. The imposing figure in the middle is none other than Sir Hubert Parry, the composer, and most of the people were singers; they were Lord Llangattock's guests on this occasion.

Opposite below: Wilderness Street in 1934. A great many streets in pre-war Bermondsey looked like this one, made up of two-storey Georgian or Victorian houses with front doors opening from the pavement and with wooden shutters to the ground-floor windows but few had such a dismal name. Wilderness Street appears as far back as Horwood's map of London in 1813. It was a short street, forming a triangle with Elim Street and Weston Street south of Long Lane.

Left: In the older parts of Bermondsey, nearer to the river, many eighteenth-century and even seventeenth-century houses survived until the Second World War. This is a view of No. 16 Curlew Street in Horselydown, just north of Tooley Street, which was described in a volume published by the Royal Commission on Historical Monuments in 1930. The front of the house bore a tablet dated 1752 but many features were much older. The door case had Corinthian pilasters, decorated with carved swags, and surmounted by scroll-brackets enclosing seated cherubs. It was a terrible pity that such splendid survivals were swept away. They would have been greatly cherished today.

Prospect Street in Rotherhithe in February 1937. The view is looking northwards, with the eastern end of Jamaica Road in the background (with the tall street lamp). The tree on the right is in Southwark Park. The side-road where the group is standing is Truman's Square and the shop in the foreground is on the corner of a side-alley called Lagos Place. All of the property on the left was demolished for the building of the Kirby Estate.

Opposite below: Thetford Place in Rotherhithe in 1934. This short cul-de-sac ran from Neptune Street to the back of Southwark Park Methodist church in Lower Road, whose circular rear window can be seen here. This was a typical nineteenth-century infill in a piece of land left after the main road had been developed and Neptune Street had been laid out. Neptune Street was named after the Neptune public house, which stood until recently on the corner of Brunel Road and Rupack Street; Neptune Street ran through from St Marychurch Street to Lower Road before the Rotherhithe Tunnel chopped it in half in the early twentieth century.

Following pages: Ainsty Street from Seth Street in Rotherhithe in January 1939. The houses in this street were severe and sparing, even for a poor Rotherhithe backstreet. There are not even any shutters to the ground-floor windows and the doorways are of the most simple sort.

Ainsty Estate in 1956. The brave new post-war world, truly worlds away from the pre-war Ainsty Street.

Adams Gardens in Rotherhithe in June 1935.

A living-room in the Adams Gardens Estate in Brunel Road in 1950. This interior would have been a revolution in comfort over a typical pre-war Bermondsey house.

Paulin Street Cottages in September 1934. Some attempt was made between the wars to build houses (or 'cottages') as opposed to blocks of flats but Government spending restrictions usually dictated otherwise.

A Bermondsey Childhood

By Barbara Stamford-Plows

I was born in 1940 in St Giles' Hospital in Camberwell during the Battle of Britain. My mother often described the incendiary bombs falling in the hospital grounds, the doctor and midwife wearing tin hats and the midwife frequently diving under the bed! I was the first child of Maud Florence and Thomas Henry Plows. They had met on a cycling club outing to Brighton and married in 1938 at St Luke's Church in Bermondsey. My father came from a large family and worked as a shop assistant at a pawnbroker's in Spa Road. In his spare time he was in the Territorial Army and so was among the first to be called up at the outbreak of war. When they were first married they lived in a basement flat in Avondale Square. The rent was 14s a week but Mum found it difficult to manage on her army allowance of 24s a week, especially when she became pregnant, so she moved to two rooms at 29 Camberwell Station Road which were only 10s a week.

When I was about eighteen months old we moved to 90 Dunton Road in Bermondsey, next door to my father's parents. The house was the second along an alley called Greyhound Terrace. It belonged to the Southern Railway and backed on to the Bricklayers Arms' Goods Yard. The engines were all steam then and were constantly shunting around. The alley was down some steps beside the road bridge that went over the lines. There were four houses, then a bombed-out pub called *The Greyhound*, then another six houses. Under the bridge was a public shelter but we never used it – we had an Anderson shelter in our back garden. At the top of the steps were big double wooden gates into the goods' yard used by the horse-drawn delivery vans. The carthorses were kept there in stables to the left of the gates. There was another large stable on the other side of the bridge on the corner of Willow Walk, which was on several levels – the horses walking up and down ramps. My earliest memory is of being held in my grandfather's arms to watch a horse and cart going in through the gates.

Grandad Plows died when I was about four, Granny Plows when I was nine. She was small and dark and walked with a limp having been run over by a tram years earlier which had left her with one leg shorter than the other. She used to sit in her kitchen behind the door and spit into the grate – it used to sizzle on the bars! There was always a peculiar smell about her, years later I discovered it was the aroma of snuff. Her kitchen was over-run with cockroaches. I remember standing by the table watching a huge cockroach run along it waving its feelers (it was at eye-level), and hearing the crunch as Granny Plows crushed it with the heel of her hand! Being infested with cockroaches sounds dreadful, but when I was a nurse they were often encountered late at night in hospital kitchens so I think that they are associated with old buildings rather than dirt. On the subject of 'livestock', I can only remember catching headlice once and this was soon dealt with by my mother with coal-tar soap and metal nit-comb whereas nowadays it seems a regular occurrence in spite of modern standards of hygiene (come back Nitty Norah – all is forgiven). I don't recall any encounter with fleas at all and the only time I ever came across bedbugs was in India. So not all of Bermondsey was a slum. We lived in an ordinary terraced house with an outside lavatory and no bathroom. Sunday night was bath night – the big zinc bath, hanging in the backyard during the week, was placed in front of the kitchen fire and filled with kettles of hot water. Then we took it in turns, youngest first, the cooling bath water topped up with another kettleful of hot water each

The view from the attic of 74 Dunton Road in 1955 looking towards the Bricklayers Arms Goods Yard.

time, sitting in front of the fire to dry our hair afterwards. I don't remember seeing the bath emptied afterwards. I suppose I must have been in bed by then but it must have been pretty heavy.

In September 1945, I started at Boutcher School in Grange Road. It was next door to St Luke's Church where my parents were married. I remember the first day quite well; I had looked forward to going and was not at all worried. I felt rather bemused by the number of other children who were crying and obviously didn't want to be there! I got a sum right and was given a postcard of three little kittens to take home – my one and only prize for arithmetic!

St Luke's Church in Grange Road in 1964 with the notice-board of the Boutcher School to the left of it. The church was demolished in the following year but the school still thrives. The buildings were opened in 1872 and were paid for by William Boutcher, a leather and hide factor, in memory of his wife who had died in 1870. To the right of the church in this view are the premises of C.E. Heinke Ltd, manufacturers of diving equipment.

This image of the Abbey Street district taken in 1946 shows a considerable number of prefabs erected in a bombed area. Abbey Street runs across the middle of the picture from left to right. The street in the right foreground is The Grange and the small street leading off it to the left (after the second prefab) is Paulin Street.

The living-room of 118 Abbey Street, a typical post-war prefab in Bermondsey in 1946.

The kitchen of 118 Abbey Street.

Abbey Buildings from Abbey Street in 1961. The tenement blocks were built in the early 1900s for the South Eastern Railway Co. These blocks were built at the junction of the then new Tower Bridge Road. Much of the site had belonged to Bermondsey Abbey in the Middle Ages; the abbey was a great Cluniac monastery which existed from 1082 to 1538 at what is now the junction of Abbey Street and Tower Bridge Road. A large church comparable with Southwark Cathedral must be imagined straddling that crossroads. These tenement blocks were demolished in the 1970s. Their site was excavated by archaeologists from the Museum of London in 1984-88. The foundations of many medieval buildings were found, chiefly from the abbey's infirmary, plus the course of the great drain which served the abbey.

Wolseley Buildings in 1949. These tenements stood in Wolseley Street in Dockhead and the view here shows the junction with Farthing Alley. The inscription high up on the wall dates them to 1883; most tenement blocks were built in the 1880s and 1890s. The name derives from Field-Marshal Sir Garnet Wolseley, the original of Gilbert and Sullivan's 'modern major-general' who led many successful campaigns in earlier years, including the Ashanti expedition of 1874 and the campaign in Egypt in 1882.

Right: Monarch Buildings in Abbey Street in 1961. These tenements stood opposite Neckinger Leather Mills and were very close to the Star Cinema.

Below: Mayflower Street in Rotherhithe in 1937. This had been Princes Street until that year. The houses dated from the eighteenth century and were decidedly superior to most of those in Rotherhithe. But they had long been used as relatively poor tenements.

Left: Mariner's Buildings in Trinity Road in Rotherhithe, *c.* 1935.

Below: Alice Street off Tower Bridge Road, photographed from Hartley's jam factory in 1934. The large domed building in the background is the Bermondsey Central Hall.

Above: Abbey Street in 1939. Note the trees, a product of Ada Salter's 'beautification' programme between the wars.

Right: Sparricks Row in 1935 showing wooden houses.

Opposite above: Alice Street in 1934.

Opposite below: Hargreave Place, off Alice Street, in 1934.

Albion Street in Rotherhithe in 1939. This is the junction with Swan Road.

A corner of Thorburn Square in 1963, not long before it was demolished to make way for blocks of flats, see below. These houses and those in all the surrounding roads had belonged to the West Estate, an extensive private estate of residential and commercial buildings which had existed since the eighteenth century. Most of its houses, however, were not built until the 1860s, when various streets were named after places lately made prominent in the Crimean War of 1854-56 (Balaclava Road, Alma Grove, Reverdy Road). The West Estate was bought by Bermondsey Borough Council in 1960. Unlike most such estates of Victorian houses, very little of it was replaced by blocks of flats so the Victorian streets are still treasured today; unfortunately its centrepiece, Thorburn Square, did suffer demolition despite its houses being much grander than the rest.

Thorburn Square redeveloped in 1963. St Anne's Church, a Victorian building (with a later hall), was retained in the centre of the square.

Mitchell & Sons shop at 96 Spa Road, *c.* 1935.

The Redriff Estate, *c.* 1959. Redriff was an alternative name for Rotherhithe and was especially popular in the seventeenth and eighteenth centuries. Pepys used it and so did Jonathan Swift when he made Captain Lemuel Gulliver a resident of the district.

three

Life and Recreation

Reminiscences

By John Caley

All youngsters had to make their own amusements and we played games in streets quite safely. Mellicks Place, close to Tower Bridge Road, was entered by descending steps at one end whilst the other end had posts allowing only hand barrows to enter. The homes had been built during the middle of the 1800s, and most of them were bug-ridden, which made life very unpleasant. At the same time children were free from the dangers of traffic and it became a playground for all. Hardly any of the games we enjoyed are played today. For the girls, skipping ropes were a must. Sometimes a larger, heavier rope enabled all to join in together. Some would put cut-out pictures into a thick book, into which other girls would stick a pin. If she hit a page containing a picture, it became hers; if not, the pin went into the spine of the book. 'Ally Gob' played with four cubes and a ball was common. Hide and seek and Tin Can Copper also kept them occupied until bed time came at around nine o'clock.

For boys, cricket and football were played around the 'hill', a sloping roadway, lined on one side by Riley Street School and at the bottom of Mellicks Place; it was rarely, if ever, entered by traffic. The main game of all the year was Release when one team hunted the other within a limited area. As boys were captured, three taps on the head making it so, they were kept in a 'box' shouting 'Release'. All played O' Grady Says under the street lamps. If you acted on all orders prefixed by the words 'O'Grady Says', it was fine but in between those who acted on an order not prefixed by O'Grady were out of the game; it was always good for a laugh.

Another was playing cards, wherein the currency wagered in 'banker' on the turn of a card was cigarette picture cards. Whilst they were mainly well-thumbed and worn, there were some new ones, and these achieved a higher value. The new cards were obtained by asking some elder person seen opening a new packet of cigarettes.

Boys and girls would make a 'grotto', usually along Tower Bridge Road; this consisted of torn-up grass fringed by a display of a few small vases, holy pictures, etc. Requests (which really were begging) made to passers-by were sometimes rewarded by a halfpenny, though at the approach of a policeman everyone connected quickly disappeared and the grotto was kicked into the gutter.

Within the street was a shop which sold everything: food of all kinds, sweets, etc. One of its attractions was a Lucky Dip, which was a tin box which held a large number of envelopes; on the inside of the flaps was written an amount ranging from ½ oz. up to 12 oz. One paid a halfpenny and thumbed the way through the envelopes in order to see one with a corner that had been slightly torn; this was an indication of a higher weight. When pulled out and examined it turned out to be ½ oz. and not a high amount. The shop keeper was too smart for us all and had got on to the trick, nullifying it by treating all envelopes the same.

Throughout the year, entertainment was brought by the various buskers including singers, some of whom were dressed as women, and performing acrobatics who danced to a barrel organ. During the summer months barrows loaded with fruits in season would appear, as did the various sellers of ice cream. Walls, Eldorado and Shules all vied for our favour at around a penny a lump. The most popular was the man who pushed a large barrow with two tubs of ice cream and remained all day at the top of the steps in Purbrook Street selling wafers of cream ice or tubs of plain ice flavoured with pieces of

Children at play on the corner of Purbrook Street in 1939.

Mellicks Place, *c.* 1935.

lemon. When he left at the end of the day he would run off the melted ice that had kept his wafers solid and generally handed out free samples of what was left, thus increasing his popularity and ensuring a regular clientele next day.

Attendance at Sunday school was rewarded with a ticket to enjoy a Christmas Party (bring your own mug). A day trip to Epping Forest was given to all at school. This meant walking from Riley Street School to Fenchurch Street Station to board a train to Loughton, then making our way to where an open-air meal of a mug of water and something to eat, provided by the Shaftesbury Society, awaited us. After this, we were free to roam the forest which lay across the road. The day ended with an impromptu sports contest, before we headed back to Fenchurch Street and trudged over to Tower Bridge and home.

The school building was not only used to educate, but also to provide leisure at holiday times and evenings; it became a play centre. On weekdays, five o'clock would see a large number of children massing around the locked gate, then at a signal given from the arches across the playground, a mad rush ensued to the foot of the stairs. All were then shepherded up in to the first-floor hall where Mrs Buchanan leant against the fireguard, rapping out orders for quiet. All lined up properly around the hall and at the call of the various classes formed a line in the centre; as the piano struck up a march, they strode off to quiet games, plasticine and cutting out, painting etc. This occupied many until seven o'clock, with a break at six o'clock for any who wished to leave. As time to go home came near, everything was packed away. The next treat was given by the person in charge who always opened a new packet of cigarettes, and whoever correctly called the number on the back of the picture in the packet became the possessor; the value of their stock of cards used in banker groups increased.

The Star Cinema in Abbey Street, *c.* 1937 showing the 'tuppenny rush'.

A feature of the streets was the various purveyors of articles of food who never missed a day. The hot pieman, with his food in a heated oven carried on a trike, made two calls nightly at 9.30 and 10.30; his pies improved when he poured warm gravy into the top of each purchase. Sunday saw the muffin man who carried a tray upon his head ringing a hand bell to announce his arrival, to be followed by a dealer in shrimps, winkles, cockles and whelks. All these eatables went to making Sunday night tea very special. Further to this, at particular times of the year, fruits of the season such as strawberries and cherries would be piled high.

If one attended Sunday school regularly, a day out to Epsom Downs was given to all attendants at St Peter's mission in Purbrook Street, Griggs Place, and St Andrew's in Abbey Street. These all came under the care of Bermondsey parish church. All met at London Bridge Station and were taken to Epsom Downs where food was given before people were free to roam at will. On returning to London Bridge in the evening, waiting their arrival was the bugle band of the 20th Bermondsey Scouts based at St Peter's mission, where band practice was held during the week. These would lead the procession of trippers along to Bermondsey Square where a service of hymns and prayers was joined by all in gratitude for a safe day out in the country.

Further to this, an annual event that attracted all of Bermondsey was the Catholic procession in the summer. Families in Mellicks Place were represented by the children who attended the Catholic schools at Dockhead, Melior Street and All Saints' in Tooley Street. The whole event was a wonderful spectacle consisting of the various guilds, bands and tableaux on carts (courtesy of Tommy Hatcher, cartage contractor). Hymns were sung as the bands played the procession through the streets on a Sunday afternoon.

In the evening, children would follow as the priest, attended by other boys, would travel the journey taken in the afternoon in order to bless the homes which had decorated the outsides as altars, attesting to their faith.

Another event which always drew youngsters was the parade of the local territorial regiment, then known as the 22nd London Regiment. A march from their base in Jamaica Road took them to Bermondsey parish church on the nearest Sunday to 11 November, Armistice Day. A special service would be held, the colours of the regiment being kept therein. This parade was supplemented when the regiment left for their annual camp; this entailed the commanding officer being mounted on a horse behind the band. Together with Nashy Hutley, a friend who had a brother in the band, we followed the band all the way to Waterloo Station by way of Dockhead, Tooley Street, London Bridge, Southwark Street and Stamford Street and creating quite a grand spectacle all the way.

Saturday mornings were given over to the 'tuppenny rush' at cinemas, the Star in Abbey Street taking pride of place. Two pictures and a serial, with a talent contest in between, were great value for 2d. However, if the screen went blank, a stamping of feet on the floors showed disappointment; people remained oblivious to all calls for 'quiet' from Mr Hart the manager, the reception of the film being greeted with loud acclaim. The talent contest was made up of brave volunteers from the audience. Some sang, some recited, some even tried to tap dance. The winner was arrived at as the recipient of the

The Drill Hall in Jamaica Road between the wars. This was the headquarters of the 22nd London Regiment (originally the 3rd Volunteer Battalion, The Queen's Royal West Surrey Regiment). To the left, there is the regimental memorial erected after the First World War, surmounted by their badge of a lamb and flag.

Old people's tea in Rotherhithe Great Hall in Lower Road in 1938. Rotherhithe Great Hall was a chapel built for Thomas Richardson in 1906. He had originally worked under the title Rotherhithe Free Church, which is also in fact the name of the present post-war church on the site. Thomas Richardson was a very successful evangelist with a strong element of social work in his programme. In addition to running his chapel, he also arranged large gatherings at the former Rotherhithe town hall on the opposite side of Lower Road.

loudest cheer as Mr Hart proceeded along the backs of the contestants and placed a hand on each head.

The afternoon show was interrupted by arguments and scuffles among the audience, yet order was quickly restored by the appearance of Mr Hart and his assistant, a middle-aged lady whose task was to sell refreshments from a tray carried before her, but whose word would silence all miscreants.

In general, Bermondsey with its tanneries, biscuit makers, tin box factories and many others like Hartley's, Crosse & Blackwell, the docks and the wharves was a place full of life and interest, even if it was just a drunk being conveyed on the two-wheeled barrow, hidden from public gaze under the concealing hood but quite happy singing at the top of his lungs (as escorted by two policemen who were in greater evidence then), approached the gates to the back yard of Tower Bridge police and of course with a following of interested boys and girls.

Rotherhithe Hippodrome in June 1931. Councillor George Stephen Tingle, the Mayor in 1930-31, attends the reopening of the building on 11 June, when 'talkies' were first shown there. The building was opened as Terriss's Theatre in 1899. It was bombed during the Second World War and the ruin was finally demolished in the 1950s.

Above: The Admiral Hawke in Jamaica Road in 1949 – another pub with a maritime name.

Opposite: Noah's Ark in Rotherhithe Street, *c.* 1928. A great many pubs in Rotherhithe bore names with maritime allusions. They were named after specific ships (the *Neptune*), naval battles (the *Battle of the Nile*), maritime trades (the *Jolly Caulkers*), or, when inspiration failed, they were just called the *Ship*. No fewer than 125 pubs are known to have existed in Rotherhithe alone.

Bermondsey schooldays in the 1920s and 1930s

By Fred Hill

Monnow Road School had one or two peculiarities. For instance, it retained the Infants' department, which I attended from 1921 at five years of age. At seven years, we were shunted off to local elementary schools, in my case to Alexis Street School nearby. When ten to eleven years old, we sat the 11-plus examination. Those who passed went to Wilson's grammar school and those who failed – as I did – went to the central school.

An idea of the curriculum may be of some interest. The school was organised into two departments. One was the technical department, which specialised in industrial subjects such as mathematics, physics, chemistry and machine drawing, for which our master in the subject, Mr Kemp, had personally acquired a whole range of car and motor cycle engines and gearboxes. French was introduced to the technical department in my second year (1927-28). To give us experience in the practical use of handtools, we had a really excellent woodwork department under Mr O'Keefe. Each boy had the personal use of a wide range of tools, his own bench and, consequently, a sense of accountability and responsibility, which with reasonable discipline and respect meant that nothing was lost, stolen or broken. We had free use of an ample supply of good quality wood, including the use of such expensive timbers as mahogany and American Black Walnut. It is perhaps ironic that in the late 1920s, when we were suffering the worst slump in the country's history, we were provided with facilities which, in this day and age, we are told we cannot afford despite the fact that we are generally so much better off. Also in my second year, we were provided with a brand-new brick-built workshop containing machine tools, including various types of lathe, machine metal saws, a smith's forge and associated items of equipment. We were taught the elements of lathe setting and operation, forging, brazing and welding, etc.

I now turn to the school's commercial department. It may sound a little odd today but in the 1920s and 1930s it was considered quite an accomplishment for boys to learn touch-typing, Gregg and Pitman shorthand and book-keeping. In the long years since then, I have sometimes considered it a wonderful asset to be able to take accurate shorthand notes at meetings particularly with the added gloss of fast and accurate touch-typing.

During my final year at the school there was an event worth recording. Due mainly to the activities of Mr Kemp, the school organised an exchange visit with a school in Hamburg. In preparation we learned a number of German semi-classical songs such as Brahms' *Lullaby* and the legendary 'Die Lorelei'; many years later, I was able to visit the area where these sirens lured unsuspecting sailors to their fate. Not unnaturally, the German boys, when they arrived, were almost obsessed with the fact that Max Schmelling had only recently won the world heavyweight boxing title. It was also a matter of interest that this exchange visit was the first organised by the two countries since the First World War. I was to have been one of the party going to Germany but the bottom fell out of my world when my father lost his job due to the imposition of import duties during the great slump. Odd too that he worked for a German-Jewish firm

Opposite: Boys in Page's Walk in 1914.

(Herzfeld's of Milk Street, E.C.), who were importers of German silks. The firm also went bust.

When the survivors of our fathers' generation returned from the First World War, they were promised 'homes fit for heroes to live in'. What they got was nothing but unremitting unemployment which developed into the most awful slump in Britain's history. It lasted from 1919 for twenty years – peaking in 1932 – the year I left school to look for a job and the year my father lost his. This terrible slump carried on until the outbreak of Hitler's war in 1939. Families were often split up by fathers being sent off to country districts for agricultural work; they would not see home for months on end. I cannot remember the name of the district, but it might have been Belmont and located in either Essex or Sussex. No generation since has experienced anything to compare. It had a tremendous effect on us – the children of that generation. For many, holidays were unknown; unemployment pay was often insufficient for food and clothing so it was not uncommon to see children in rags ('ragged-arsed' in the terminology of the time). Many wore shoes where the soles had parted company with the uppers, and sometimes without socks. Any ideas of Christmas or birthday presents remained dreams. Children had to make their own.

The most successful of these were the home-made scooters based on a piece of old floor board for the base and another for the steering column. The steering swivel was

German schoolboys outside Bermondsey town hall in 1930. They were there as part of the exchange referred to by Fred Hill.

Tanner Street recreation ground in 1938.

made from a wood block measuring about 3ins by 3ins by 8ins, fixed to the base with 3in nails. Two screw eyes went into the vertical front of the steering block, matched with two more in the steering column. Two worn car ball bearings had to be obtained from a repairing garage to make the wheels. Fortunately in the 1920s many cobble stone, granite sett and tarred block roads were being resurfaced with asphalt, giving a beautifully smooth surface for our ball-bearing scooters.

Footballs were far too expensive, so lads of my day made their own from tightly rolled newspapers shaped into a ball then tied with strong cord or string. Girls confined themselves to games such as hopscotch, using balls of chalk to scribe the hopscotch form or pitch on the pavements.

Many cigarette manufacturers put artistic give-away cards in their packets which could be collected to make up sets of anything from regiments of the British army to wild flowers, and then pasted into albums. Boys used them for a different purpose. Four or five boys would gather with their stocks of cards, and one card would be stood at an angle to an external house wall. The players would stand at the kerb and take turns to flick one of their cards at the target. If they missed, their card would remain on the pavement. When a boy succeeded in hitting the target, he would then win all the cards lying on the pavement.

Redriff Rowing Club in 1950. Miss Eileen Greenwood, the Mayor of Bermondsey, presents a cup to the Redriff Rowing Club Four. The club had won the National Dock Labour Board Trophy for 1950.

Bermondsey Women's Club outing in 1954.

The Municipal Club in the Solarium in Grange Road in 1959.

Memories of Great Dover Street and its vicinity

By Joyce and Fred Newman

In Great Dover Street before Dewrance & Co. extended their premises, there was the Brunswick Chapel, which my wife used to attend to see lantern slides and get a bowl of soup and a bun before the Second World War. My wife and her sister attended school each Sunday and lantern slides each Wednesday. Her sister got married in St Andrew's Church in New Kent Road in June 1944 – just as an air-raid warning started. All the guests except the cats' meat lady from Great Dover Street ran away to the air-raid shelters and did not return for the wedding breakfast, so most of the food was given to the black American troops who were passing by Great Dover Street in convoy on the way to the coast. About this time too, the family had to stand in the sandbag shelter under the railway bridge near the cinemas in New Kent Road all night, having been turned off a bus during another raid. Then they got home to find that a land mine had flattened the Virginia Plant public house in Great Dover Street opposite Black Horse Court. Dolcis' shoe factory was where the new flats are being built in Great Dover Street. The Metal Box Co. was behind it.

My wife and I were married in the crypt of Trinity Church in October 1945, because St Andrew's Church was unsafe.

There were two cinemas at the crossroads of Great Dover Street, New Kent Road, Old Kent Road and Tower Bridge Road: the Globe and Old Kent picture houses. In the latter I saw a film with Jack Hulbert and Cicely Courtneidge in which they sang *The flies crawl up the window.* In Old Kent Road there was the German butcher's on the High Pavement where on a Saturday night they used to sell joints etc. at cheaper prices, swinging and slapping the same and shouting, 'Buy, buy, buy now'.

Also along the left-hand side was a dairy where it was rumoured that any lettuce and vegetables left on a plate by diners were collected, washed and reserved. Stalls in Sayer Street near the Elephant and Castle sold eels whose bodies could be seen wriggling about – their heads had been chopped off. These stalls were lit by gaslight. On foggy days around the Elephant and Castle, trams used to follow men with lighted sticks and the middle open rail was dangerous to a cyclist trying to cross the lines, as at any time the front wheel could slip down the gap and throw the cyclist over the handlebars.

A No.68 tram in Jamaica Road in June 1951. This photograph was taken from St James's Church and therefore the tram is in the present Old Jamaica Road. No.68 went down Tower Bridge Road and via Bricklayers' Arms towards Waterloo Station. In the other direction, it went to Greenwich. The entire journey was scheduled to take thirty-four minutes. Waterloo to Surrey Docks took twenty-four minutes. The sharp bends at Dockhead slowed down this route and the No.70 from London Bridge. Until the early 1960s, the main road from Tooley Street to St James's Church passed St Saviour's Dock and then took a turn to the left into the street called Dockhead before making more than a ninety-degree turn to the right into Parkers Row. Then it crossed the line of the present Jamaica Road to make a big loop south of it, skirting the drill hall and war memorial on the corner with Abbey Street to arrive close by the north wall of St James's Church before joining the existing route towards Rotherhithe Tunnel.

The last tram in July 1952. Robert Mellish, the Member of Parliament for Bermondsey, joins the crew and a great many passengers in observing the last tram. The double-deck tram was one of London's most familiar sights for some fifty years and their removal in 1952 amounted to a huge change in London life.

Methodist Church Life

By John Beasley

Bermondsey Central Hall

The inspiring story of Bermondsey Central Hall features prominently in *The Bitter Cry Heard and Heeded: The Story of the South London Mission of the Methodist Church 1889-1989* which I had the privilege of writing for the Mission's centenary. I remember in the 1960s going into the huge hall which held over 2,000 people and was filled for Sunday services after the central hall opened in 1900.

As a Methodist local preacher I have had various experiences in Bermondsey central hall. In different services, I have witnessed a mouse run across the floor, police messages being heard on the loud speaker system and an organist falling asleep – not during the sermon – and having to be woken up so we could sing a hymn.

The worst experience I had in the Central Hall was when I was the last person to leave after a Sunday evening service and found myself locked in – trapped between the outside door and the inner security door. I had to shout through the door and ask a passer-by to phone the police. I now have a fear of being trapped in buildings because of that experience along with being accidentally locked in a building in Slovakia.

Lord Soper at Galleywall Road

Lord Soper who started his ministry at Oakley Place Wesleyan church in 1926 attended the centenary celebrations of the South London Mission at Manor Methodist church in Galleywall Road in 1989. There he told the story of when he was arrested at Tower Hill in 1979. A young police officer accused the veteran campaigner of causing an obstruction. So the seventy-six-year-old Lord was ordered to get down from his platform.

As Donald Soper had been speaking at Tower Hill virtually every week since 1926, he refused to obey the police officer's instruction. The constable then arrested him and told Lord Soper to wait for a police van.

Soon a senior police officer arrived and apologised for the mistake in arresting him. Lord Soper, intrigued to know what would happen to the constable, asked: 'Will he be punished?' The senior police officer replied: 'No, he will be informed'.

The World Turned Upside Down, Old Kent Road, early twentieth century. This and the picture on page 82 come from just outside Bermondsey but the Old Kent Road has always been a great influence on the district. It was nothing if not a drinking street and this is one of its best-known pubs.

The Swan Lane festival in the summer of 1951. The Member of Parliament for Bermondsey,
Robert Mellish, stands on the left, and on the right is Alfred John Kemp, the Mayor of Bermondsey
from 1951-52.

Pearlies at St Mary Magdalene's in Massinger Street off the Old Kent Road in 1938. The Old Kent Road and Walworth were famous for their costermongers but Bermondsey harboured many in Tower Bridge Road and Southwark Park Road. The Pearlies developed as a charitable body within the costermongers' communities. Between the wars they were attracted to St Mary Magdalene's Church in Massinger Street by its Vicar, Alfred William Barker, who was popularly known as 'the Bishop of the Old Kent Road' (and also 'the Cockney Parson'). After the church was closed and demolished, the Pearlies went to Bermondsey parish church in Bermondsey Street, another and much more venerable St Mary Magdalen's.

four

Dire Poverty

From Silver Watch to Lovely Black Eye

These extracts from Cyril Bustin's memoir of the above title, reflect a world of dire poverty. Cyril Bustin went to work in 1927 as an Assistant Relieving Officer under the old Poor Law in its closing years. Until 1930, the local relief of poverty was the responsibility of the Bermondsey Board of Guardians. This was the same body which had run the Tanner Street workhouse and the Parish Street workhouse next to St John's churchyard. Bermondsey may have been a hive of industry and enterprise but wages were low before the Second World War and many people lacked work (or sufficient work). Cyril Bustin was also a life-long worker at the Bermondsey Gospel Mission, of which he was eventually the Superintendent from 1946 to 1962. His parents, William and Annie Bustin, had run the establishment from 1891 to 1946. His mother was widely known as Madam Annie Ryall because of her role as a Gospel singer. Annie Ryall's father, Walter Ryall, had been its founder as far back as 1864.

Applications for relief

Bermondsey had two Board of Guardians' offices; one for Bermondsey, the other for Rotherhithe, my appointment being to the former, situated in Tooley Street in Dockhead

Above: Cyril Bustin and his wife pictured at the Bermondsey Gospel Mission.

Opposite: Arnolds Place in January 1936.

The Bermondsey Gospel Mission building on the corner of Abbey Street and Old Jamaica Road in 1976.

end. While the entrance to the offices was in the main road, applicants for help used the entrance in Shad Thames, crossing a large paved yard. There were four Relieving Officers, each having responsibility for a quarter of the borough. It was to one of these that I went as assistant. The office was an individual room leading out of the passage, the other three Relieving Officers occupying similar. Applicants were not invited into the room since they may leave unwelcome visitors in the way of fleas and bugs. They were therefore interviewed by way of a small window at the side, by which there was stuck a poster warning of prosecution for false statements, with the number where action had been taken over the past two or three months. Upon help being asked, name and address were taken, and a visit made not only to check residence by means of rent book but also to see if there was any article of furniture that could be sold to meet the need and to examine cupboards or other hiding place where food was likely to be hidden. Being satisfied, the person would then be told to attend the office when they were supplied with food tickets for the purpose of getting a loaf of bread or butter-beans or the like.

Slum court

We sometimes see the newspaper placards proclaiming a social security fraud crackdown. Even in the days of the Poor Law, there was fraud. Many claimants for relief did casual work such as late-night portering at London Bridge Station. The Relieving Officers would go there from time to time to watch out for their claimants.

One day my boss said he would be taking a walk up to London Bridge Station late in the evening and agreed to my going with him. At 11.30 p.m. we met at the corner of Abbey Street but instead of going up Parkers Row, we went by way of Arnolds Place, just a paved court-way, and even out of this there was a small court of several cottages. We were a little surprised to find one of our very elderly clients, a man, sitting in an armchair. Asking the reason, there came the reply, 'Can't sleep indoors tonight, the bugs have taken over'. Leaving him to sleep it out, we went on and finished our journey. Visits to the homes were frequent and it was not long before it was the turn of our late-night friend to have a call. What I found was a couple of rooms with only the bare necessities, and with no home-helps in those days, the rooms were in a filthy state. People in those days did not need to lock doors so you just knocked by using the knocker if there happened to be one. Going into the room into which the street door led, there lying on a broken-down couch was the client, who was covered head to foot with bugs small and large. It was not possible to get rid of them once and for all, even when fumigated since every cottage had its share and the bugs did not mind whose cottage they lived in so long as there was some human to live and feed on. It was therefore necessary for an inspection on

William Bustin and his wife at the laying of the foundation stone of the Silver Walk flats in 1922.

The Board of Guardians' offices in Tooley Street in 1898. The Boards of Guardians were set up under the Poor Law Amendment Act of 1834. In the case of Bermondsey, the parishes of St Olave, St John and St Thomas were put together as the St Olave's Union on 1 February 1836. The parishes of Bermondsey and Rotherhithe remained independent of the union and of each other until 1869. There was then a re-arrangement of workhouses with the result that the old Rotherhithe workhouse in Lower Road was made the infirmary or hospital of the Union. That is why a hospital in Lower Road came to have the name of a church next to London Bridge Station. The St Olave's Board of Guardians was renamed the Bermondsey Board of Guardians in 1904. When the Poor Law was wound up in 1930, its duties were taken over by the London County Council.

arriving home at the end of the working day; the main place for examination being the turn-ups of one's trousers. There were plenty of fleas around at that time so that what was called 'a small-tooth comb' had to come into play from time to time.

Fiddling

A married couple living in Maze Pond, hard by Guy's, were receiving assistance for themselves and seven children and had been for a long time. Each time a visit was made, only the very young children were there. Telling the father that a visit would be made on the Saturday and he was to present the seven, the day arrived and there were the seven. Upon my asking a question he turned to one child, whose reply was to have been 'Yes, Dad' as the others had said, but the game was up since the children of school age had been gathered in from the neighbours.

Maze Pond in
February 1937.

Additional earnings

There was the case of a man with two wives living in two upstairs rooms in the
converted Parish Street workhouse. He was receiving assistance for himself and his wife,
the other being a prostitute. Having made a visit one day, the man and wife being out,
this lady was in and the method of invitation told all I wished to know at that moment
other than where she was living. She gave no address but denied living there. Making an
early call the next morning and being kept waiting, I knew something was hastily being
arranged. The door was opened and I stepped into the hall, the bedroom door being open
for my benefit; I was able to see it was empty except behind the door. They were quite
willing for me to look but I had no success. In the hall there was a cupboard. Making my
way to it the woman, screaming obscene language, stood with her back to the door with
arms outstretched – 'you are not looking in there' – but ultimately giving way, the door
opened. All to be seen at first was a pile of coal, but there round the side was the lady
concerned, still in her nightdress.

Devon Mansions
(formerly Hanover
Buildings) in 1976.
This block is opposite
Sweeney Crescent.

Pathos

In the top attic room of a four-story house in Tanner Street lived a woman with lupus
covering the whole side of her face; she attended Guy's Hospital for X-ray treatment.
Visiting, it was necessary to climb up narrow flights of stairs with no banister. On the
way up, hearing two voices, I assumed she had a visitor, but getting into the room I
found her to be alone. In the room, apart from the usual muddle and muck, there were
three large wooden chests. Getting permission, I was able to examine one, though in
those days general inspection was expected. On the second visit, some weeks later, again I
heard the double conversation. In view of the state of the woman's health, I arranged for
a health visit, with the result that all the boxes were examined. This solved the mystery,
for in one was the person with whom she had held her conversations, the skeleton of her
illegitimate baby.

Investigation

One day, standing about in the office with nothing to do, I said to the boss, 'I'm going to pick out a case at random to investigate'. Having no such things as filing cabinets, the case papers were just lined up on a shelf. Picking one out, the boss asked the name, and upon my saying who it was, his reply was, 'You will get nothing on him'. 'Well, I'll have a go since it is a family that has been on for a very long time'. 'Well,' said the boss, 'if you find anything, I'll give you five shillings for your kid's outing (Band of Hope) next week'. Studying every detail of the case, it being a very thick one, I soon made a start investigating the next morning. It so happened the family lived opposite the office some floors up in Hanover Buildings (now Devon Mansions), the family consisting of man, wife, and one young daughter at work. My first approach was a visit to the flat; normally in these flats, the street door opened directly into the room, but not in this one for a curtain rod had been fitted so that it was possible to be in the room but not see all of it. Having finished the interview, my next line of action was to visit the daughter's place of work which was an envelope factory in Bermondsey Square. Confirming her minimum wage, I asked about any overtime, the reply being that she does not do any on the premises but she takes work home, bringing it back in the morning. 'Does it amount to very much', I asked. 'Yes', was the answer, 'much more than she could manage herself; she must have help'. I ended the interview, having noticed when inspecting office records, that the man of the family had had a post as chauffeur; I did think it strange that such a man had not reported at least a casual job at any time. So making my way to the West End, I went to the offices of the AA where they were asked if the man was known to them. Getting a negative reply, it was suggested I try the RAC, and it was there I got my answer. Yes, he was known. He worked for them as a courier at weekends in Paris. Needless to say, I went back to the office to collect my five shillings for the outing and left the case to a higher authority to deal with.

Stranger than fiction

One might say my next case was stranger than fiction; again it was in a top attic. As had happened many times before, the people I went to see were out. I knocked on the next door for any information. 'Come in', was the call. This was what I saw: a room chock-a-block, a single bed just away from the door to let one get in that far, then a little gap by which one was able to get into the centre, but only just. Squatting on the floor was what looked like a gorilla bending over a small oil stove on the floor with peelings of some sort. When the man, for man it was, looked up, he was wearing a black garment covering from neck to feet and had a large bushy black beard and hair looking like a door-mat. Except for around the bed, the rest of the room was covered with white dust. Along the wall on one side of the room about 2ft wide there were piled hundreds of books. Explaining who I was, I asked if he was in need of financial assistance. 'No', was the reply. I asked if I may look at the books. 'You may', came the reply 'but they are covered in dust and I don't expect they will be of interest to you, being all theological'. Having satisfied my inquisitiveness and thanking the gentleman, I left wondering what I had found. Telling of the encounter back at the office, I found he was known to my boss and here is the story. He was the Revd George Martin of St George's Church at the top of Long Lane but had been defrocked. Walking along Cheapside and coming to an art shop, he had seen

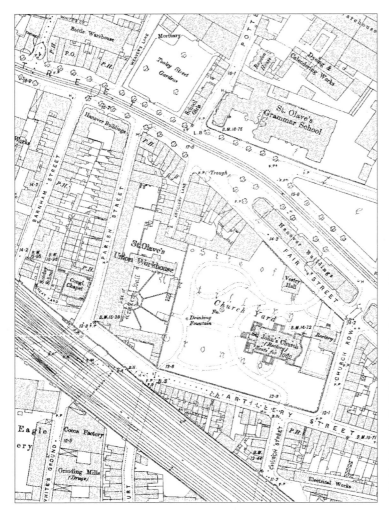

Parish Street workhouse (St Olave's Union workhouse) shown on a 60ins Ordnance Survey map of 1894-96. The Parish Street workhouse originally served the parishes of St Olave and St John. The map also shows one of the blocks of Hanover Buildings, the church of St John in Horselydown and the railway lines approaching London Bridge Station.

a painting of a nude in its window. He went into the shop and asked for its removal from the window. This being refused, he went outside, picked up a brick, and threw it through the plate-glass window. For this, he was reprimanded. At a later date, there was to be a procession passing through the Borough High Street. The church authority had given permission for stands to be erected in the forecourt of the church, which Mr Martin did not agree with. He therefore burnt them down. Being defrocked, he took the top attic room, transferring his library of several hundred books with him. Not to be outdone, he continued to wear the frock and acted privately as 'vicar' to the Borough Market. I found out that there were relatives living in Cornwall from whom he was able to get cash, but restricting the amount, knowing most of it would be given away. The day I next saw him, he was confined to bed, and on the small table beside him was a lovely cooked meal of fish provided by tradesmen of the market who had taken him as their very own padre.

five

Municipal and Political Bermondsey

Commemoration of Bermondsey's fallen of the First World War in April 1920. The Bishop of
Southwark, Dr Cyril Garbett (later Archbishop of York), gives a blessing at the unveiling of
the temporary cenotaph in West Lane in Rotherhithe on 21 April 1920. The Mayor in this
photograph, who unveiled the cenotaph, is William Bustin. He served as Mayor from 1919–22. He
was also the Superintendent of the Bermondsey Gospel Mission (see Chapter 4).

The permanent municipal war memorial in West Lane in October 1921. The spot chosen for the memorial was the very wide pavement on the eastern side of that street, where the millstream ran until the beginning of the twentieth century. The memorial was unveiled on 8 October 1921 by a local woman, Mrs Speer, who had lost three sons in the war. At one time the main road towards Deptford ran along Jamaica Road, turned left into West Lane, and then crossed Mill Pond Bridge into Paradise Street at the back of this view.

Above: Dr Alfred Salter, the Member of Parliament for Bermondsey, and Charles Ammon, the Member of Parliament for Camberwell North, at a temperance meeting in 1937. Despite his disapproval of alcohol, Salter told the story against himself in which, as a medical doctor, he informed a patient that he had just six months to live. Eighteen months later, Salter was astonished to see the patient looking quite well. The patient explained that his 'sentence' had driven him to drink and that the drink had apparently cured him! On another occasion, Dr Salter defied the uproar caused when he accused the House of Commons of harbouring many drunks. A compliment that would have brought a wry smile to Salter's face came from a Bermondsey docker, who was reported as saying 'He's got guts', to which sentiment he promptly raised his glass! Salter's strictures on the bibulous Commons were jocularly brushed aside by the then Father of the House, T.P. O'Connor. He recounted the story of William Pitt the Younger who was told by a parliamentary friend that he could not see the Speaker. Pitt replied: 'I can see three Speakers!'

Previous pages: Staff of the public health department in 1927. Dr Richard King Brown, the then Medical Officer of Health, is sitting in the middle of the second row from the front.

Dr D.M. Connan, the Medical Officer of Health in 1930. Donald Murray Connan first came to Bermondsey in 1920 as the medical officer to the tuberculosis clinic. He was appointed Medical Officer of Health in 1928. In his time, Bermondsey Borough Council pursued a vigorous programme to improve public health whose centrepiece was the opening of the public health centre in Grange Road in 1937. Dr Connan was especially notable for his work in promoting public health through films in collaboration with H.W. Bush. In 1935 he wrote *A History of the Public Health Department in Bermondsey*, which was his thesis for the degree of doctor of medicine. He remained in office until 1957 and died a few months later aged sixty-seven.

Alexandra Rose Day in 1938. For many decades, this was one of the most popular 'flag days' throughout London. It was named in 1912 in commemoration of the fiftieth anniversary of the arrival in England of Queen Alexandra (1844-1925), the wife of King Edward VII (reigned 1901-10). She arrived in London via Bricklayers Arms station in the Old Kent Road, which was a passenger station until the 1860s. Money collected on Alexandra Rose Day was used for hospitals. Collectors are seen here in 1938 on the steps of the town hall in Spa Road with the Mayor, Councillor Albert Mansell Downing.

The opening of Tanner Street recreation ground in 1929. In this photograph, Dr Alfred Salter, the Member of Parliament for Bermondsey, and his wife Ada, plant a tree to commemorate the opening of the recreation ground, which had been the site of Bermondsey workhouse. To plant a tree was particularly appropriate for Ada Salter, who was a leading proponent of improving Bermondsey's streets through tree-planting. She served for years as Chairman of the Beautification Committee (surely one of the most extraordinary titles a council committee has ever had), which oversaw considerable efforts to brighten the borough between the wars. In support of the Salters in this picture were Alderman Andrew Amos, the rector of St Mary's at Rotherhithe (to the right of Ada Salter); Ben Smith, the Member of Parliament for Rotherhithe and later a minister under Attlee (to the right of Alfred Salter); and the Mayor of Bermondsey in 1929-30, George Alfred Horwood (wearing the chain). The opening took place on Saturday 11 May 1929. Tanner Street had once been called Russell Street and before that was known as Five Foot Lane. The workhouse was first built there in the eighteenth century. During the First World War it was partly known as the King Albert Hospital for Belgian Soldiers. Many Belgian refugees came to England at that time; this country had declared war on the Kaiser's Germany in 1914 because the latter had broken a treaty of Belgian neutrality. A public house in Tooley Street, which had long been called the King of Prussia, was renamed the King of Belgium at the outbreak of war. Unfortunately its name has been changed in recent years.

Above: Alderman Edward Snowdon, the Chairman of Bermondsey's safety committee, handing out copies of the Highway Code at Pearce Duff's in 1950. He had served as Mayor in 1949-50.

Right: James D. Stewart, FLA, in 1930. He was Bermondsey's chief librarian from 1923-50. He is known chiefly for his account of Bermondsey in the Second World War, which was written in the immediate aftermath but was not published until 1980 by the old Bermondsey and Rotherhithe Society under the title of *Bermondsey in War.* Two extracts from it appear in Chapter 6.

Percy Clare, MBE in 1956. He served as the chief librarian of the borough of Bermondsey from 1950 until the borough ceased to exist in 1965. By then he had worked in the libraries' service for forty-five years. During the Second World War, however, in common with many of the council's officers, he was transferred into war work. The wartime borough librarian, J.D. Stewart (see above) was appointed Deputy Food Officer in the Bermondsey Food Office and thereafter his senior staff came from the local public libraries. In 1942, after Stewart had been asked by the government to undertake duties at the Ministry of Food's headquarters, he was succeeded by Percy Clare as Bermondsey's Deputy Food Officer. For his service in that role, Percy Clare was awarded the MBE. Bermondsey's central library was in Spa Road, next to the town hall, from 1892-1965; the building remained a library in the present London Borough of Southwark until 1989. The picture on the wall in this photograph shows the various municipal buildings in Spa Road, of which the library is the one on the far left.

The public health cinema van in 1937. A great many of the films shown were aimed at children telling them, for example, to brush their teeth properly.

Above: The Mayor of Bermondsey, Cllr Eileen Greenwood, is piped aboard HMS *Redriff* at Stave Yard in the Surrey Commercial Docks in 1950. Many ships plied Bermondsey's docks and wharves in the past and it was for long a part of the municipal round to make visits to them and, in the case of the Royal Navy, to foster special connections. HMS *Quadrant* was adopted by the borough in the Second World War.

Right: Badge of HMS *Quadrant* in 1942. This badge was presented by the Admiralty to Bermondsey council to commemorate the adoption of the ship by the borough during Warship Week in 1942. The connection continued after the Second World War. On one occasion, Bermondsey's Registrar of Births, Marriages and Deaths, Miss Grace Myers, attended a reception for the ship's company at Portsmouth. She who had married some 600 couples in her work promptly fell for a Chief Petty Officer and duly married him at Portsmouth in 1951. The badge is now kept in Bermondsey parish church.

A Bermondsey book is donated to a library in California in 1951. In that year, Bermondsey Borough Council donated Volume II of the *Defensiones Theologiae Thomas Aquinatis* by Johannes Capreolus, to the Henry E. Huntington library in San Marino in California. The volume was a work of medieval theology printed at Venice in 1483. It had been discovered that the Huntington library held three of the four volumes making up the set, and that Bermondsey's odd volume would supply the gap. The decision was therefore made to donate the volume to San Marino. The above picture shows the ceremony in California on 23 July 1951 when the British Consul-General in Los Angeles, R.H. Hadow (holding the book), handed it to Dr Robert A. Millikan, the Chairman of the library's Board of Trustees. An interesting detail of the event is that one of the trustees pictured, seventh from the left, is Dr Edwin P. Hubble, the famous astronomer, after whom a space telescope has since been named. Hubble made his name by showing that galaxies were moving away from each other at enormous speeds and that the universe was therefore expanding. Yet here he is dealing with an obscure work of theology from the Middle Ages. He died in 1953.

Grange Road Baths

By Barbara Stamford-Plows

My father went to the public baths in Grange Road and from the age of about ten I went there too every Friday night after school. It was lovely; I think it was a penny if you took your own soap and towel or you could pay extra to use theirs. Sometimes I had a bath cube to crumble into the water to make it smell nice. The tap was operated by the attendant outside and you had to call out 'more hot in No.6', etc. I was too shy at first to call out so must have endured a few lukewarm baths before I got used to it.

Grange Road baths pictured between the wars. They were opened in September 1927 in succession to the original Victorian baths in Spa Road.

Above: The presentation of the Bermondsey mace in 1954. Sir Harry Methven, the head of W.S. Shuttleworth & Co. Ltd, the well-known firm of chocolate manufacturers in Galleywall Road, gave a silver-gilt mace to the borough of Bermondsey in 1954; when the Queen had visited in her Coronation year – 1953 – Bermondsey had needed to borrow a mace. The ceremony shown here was its presentation in the town hall in Spa Road on 20 September by the Lord Mayor of London, Sir Noel Bowater. During the ceremony when the leader of Bermondsey council referred to the borough's motto, 'Craftsmanship profits the people', the lights went out.

Right: The dedication service for the mace in 1954. After the ceremony in the town hall, a dedication service was held in St Mary Magdalen's Church (Bermondsey parish church). Four trumpeters of the Life Guards added much pomp to the proceedings. St Mary Magdalen's Church stood next to Bermondsey Abbey in the Middle Ages. It did not have a daughter-church until St James's was opened in 1829. Many more local churches were built during the nineteenth century.

Horses in Bermondsey

By Barbara Stamford-Plows

There were lots of horses in Bermondsey then – railway vans, Carter Paterson, council dustcarts, coal carts, United Dairies, Price's bread vans, greengrocers, rag and bone man, and even a privately owned gig with a high-stepping chestnut pony. Even in the early 1950s, the streets were littered with straw and oats and you could often get a shovel-full of horse manure for the rhubarb. I knew all the local horses and always carried pieces of stale bread to give them on the way to school. One day I was allowed to drive the bread van, which wasn't really very exciting as the pony knew his route and just ambled along stopping at all his usual places and not taking any notice of me at all – but I was still very happy.

Bermondsey Borough Council had horse-drawn dustcarts and for a time we all used to go round to the stables in Neckinger after school to help with the feeds and stand on upturned buckets to groom them. Sometimes we used to go and play in some bombed-out houses in Alscot Road or Keyse Road, daring each other to cross a room balancing on the joists. Eventually my father stopped me from going to the council stables. He didn't explain why, whether it was because I was getting home later and later from school or whether he was afraid that something else was going on, I never found out. Anyway, I stopped going. In those days, if your parents said 'don't', you didn't.

A farewell to a Bermondsey Borough Council horse in May 1953. The Stable Superintendent Mr J. Page, and some of his drivers, made their farewell to James, one of the council's horses replaced by motor vehicles in 1953. Bermondsey had kept its municipal horses longer than the neighbouring boroughs but horses in commercial use remained fairly numerous until the 1960s.

The mayor and town clerk. The Mayor of Bermondsey in this picture is Cllr F.J. Ackland who served in 1960–61 and the town clerk is J.S. Lambert. This is the quintessential view of the dignified tier of local government as it used to be, with a mayor chosen from the political world but standing apart from it during his year of office and the equally detached town clerk who was almost always a lawyer.

Cllr Mrs Evelyn Coyle in May 1962. She served as Mayor of Bermondsey in 1962–63 and is seen here wearing the mayoral chain with its symbols of the constituent areas of the borough: a ship for Rotherhithe, a lion with a crozier for Bermondsey, and a crown and axe for St Olave's. Mrs Coyle had served as a councillor from 1931 and had represented the council on a great many committees. She died in 1974.

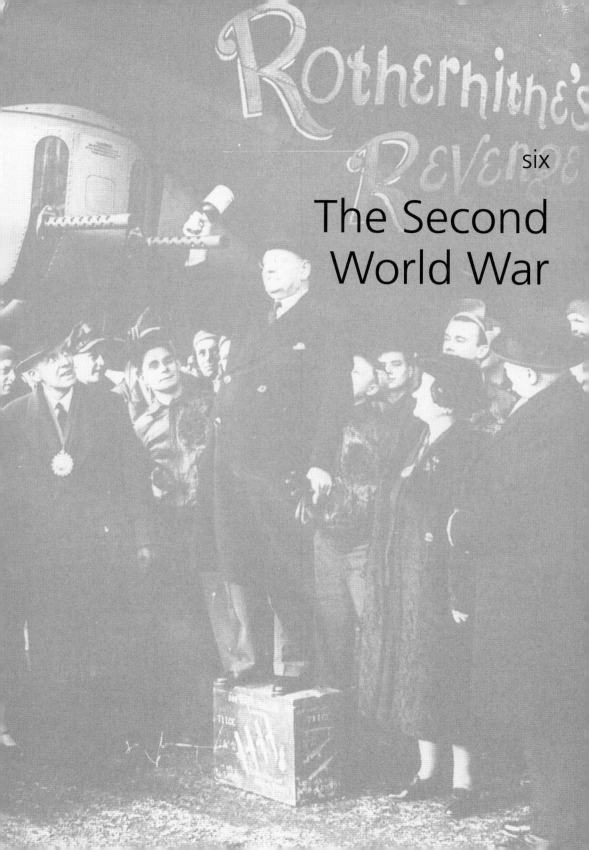

six

The Second World War

Memories of the Blitz

By Brenda Victoria (Vickie) Roffe née Moore

I was born in Guy's Hospital in 1936 and lived with my parents William and Mary Moore in Weston Street. I have no recollection of the place as with the coming of the motor vehicle, we had to move. Dad had to take his beloved horses, Mary and Bess, to the slaughterhouse and this upset Dad for days for he was very fond of them. My sister told me that at a street party in 1937 Dad turned up on his horse and cart, a photographer saw them and as a result he was in the newspaper with the headlines, 'The uninvited guest'.

We went to live in the Surrey Docks in Rotherhithe and my first memory was of the Blitz. The docks were being bombed really badly one night and we were all told to leave our homes. Being a small child I was hoisted up on a friend's shoulders, so I had a bird's eye view of all the boats ablaze. I remember Dad out on the burning boats, helping to get people off. We were told to get out through the docks and crowds of people were trying to get out of the area. I don't recall anymore about the docks but I remember going to a school and sleeping in a cloakroom with bombs dropping all around us and the building rattled all night long. Years later, mother told me the school we were in was in Deptford High Street. Apparently, because there were so many people, we were divided between two schools. I don't know the name of the other school, but it received a direct hit and nobody survived. Later we found out that a neighbour Mrs Murphy and her large family of boys had been killed. Because of the war we left Bermondsey to stay with an aunt in Dagenham. We were then given a home there and never returned to live in Bermondsey.

Although we lived in Dagenham, we did come back to see our Granny Cosson who lived in Camberwell. She was a quaint old lady and I remember her for taking snuff. Her nose was always stained brown. She would never use the electric lights, put in by the landlord, and always used her gas lights. She would read her papers with a large magnifying glass. I often went to the off-licence nearby to get her jug filled up with Guinness.

Sandbags at Bermondsey Central Baths in Grange Road in September 1939. At the beginning
of the Second World War, huge numbers of sandbags were placed around the entrances to many
buildings. In this case, Bermondsey Central Baths in Grange Road, opposite the junction with Spa
Road, was substantially protected against bomb blasts. The baths were demolished in 1975.

Civil Defence personnel. The Civil Defence Controller was William E. Baker, OBE. Under him came numerous branches of the service, the wardens, light and heavy rescue, the fire guard, first aid posts etc. He had two staff officers, John Blake and J. Bickel (see succeeding pictures) who appear here in the front row, third from the left and extreme right. Many people who had held senior peacetime appointments were given important responsibilities in the Civil Defence. In the middle of the back row in this group is Dr C.H.C. Toussaint, the Deputy Medical Officer of Health. To the right of him is H.W. Bush who ran the film programme of the public health department for many years.

Left: John Blake GM MBE. He served as a staff officer in Bermondsey's wartime Civil Defence organisation under the controller. He was awarded the George Medal for rescue work on 7 September 1940, at the very beginning of the Blitz. John Blake was to be appointed Bermondsey Borough Council's establishment officer in 1954, a considerable promotion from his original municipal role as a dustman. He died in 1959.

Below: An anti-aircraft battery was established on the Oval in Southwark Park in 1939. Rocket-firing guns were kept there.

Right: J.M. Bickel, who had normally worked in Bermondsey Borough Council's accounts' department, pictured in his Civil Defence uniform during the Second World War. He served as a staff officer under the controller.

Below: During the Second World War the Women's Voluntary Service (later the Women's Royal Voluntary Service or WRVS) contributed to Bermondsey's Civil Defence by running a van such as this called an Incident Inquiry Point or I.I.P. One van, for example, was placed in Monnow Road in 1944 to help in the aftermath of the first V2 attack on Bermondsey. One of the deadly rockets had landed near the John Bull Arch, carrying the railway line across Southwark Park Road on 26 October. A second V2 landed on the same arch on 5 November 1944.

Right: Mrs E. Bruin, a wartime fire guard officer in Bermondsey.

Below: Bermondsey Women's Voluntary Service in 1944.

Above: Mrs E. Bruin on the left, and Mrs Bidell the American Ambassador's wife, standing next to one of the London County Council's ambulances outside Peter Hills' Infant School, *c.* 1940.

Opposite: Stainer Street Arch in 1941. Many people sheltered under the railway viaduct running out of London Bridge Station during the war on the false assumption that its great solidity and strength would protect them better than an ordinary shelter. However, bombs had a tremendous penetrating force and they could easily break through a viaduct to explode with terrible effect in the enclosed space beneath. Stainer Street Arch was a very long arch because it lay underneath London Bridge Station and in the Blitz it housed a Medical Aid Post at its southern end. At 10.25 p.m. on 17 February 1941, a high-explosive bomb exploded in the Medical Aid Post near St Thomas's Street. At least sixty-eight people were killed and 175 injured. No remains were found of a number of people thought to have been in the arch at the time. This was one of the worst wartime incidents in Bermondsey.

Bermondsey in the Blitz

By James D. Stewart

The following two extracts are taken from the Bermondsey borough librarian's account of the district during the war.

I told you it was a bomb!

A very heavy bomb which dropped in the Hawkstone Road and Rotherhithe New Road triangle levelled the surrounding houses and left a huge crater about 60ft in diameter. Perched on the edge of this crater the rescue party found an Anderson shelter, partly covered with earth. When the escape hatch was opened, an elderly lady emerged and surveyed the scene, Then bending down to the hatch, she said, 'There you are Emily – I told you it was a bomb!'

Left with a door-knob

One evening during the Blitz, a bomb demolished some shops and a public house in Abbey Street. Shortly afterwards, a member of the 'Abbey Street Squad' (a name that will bring back memories to a number of people) was seen wandering in a dazed condition holding a large and ornamental door-knob. When asked what had happened to him he replied: 'Well, I was just going into the King John's Head when there was a hell of a bang and I was left with this in my hand!'

Memories of the war

By Cyril Bustin

The onset of the Blitz

Air-raid warnings were fairly frequent in London in the summer of 1940 but it was 7 September when Bermondsey really did learn what bombing was like. It so happened that on that day my wife, self and daughter, aged twelve years, were spending the day with a relative at Welling when the siren sounded. Not having the faintest idea what awaited us, we departed, taking a bus. Travelling over Shooters Hill and arriving at the top, we had a panoramic view of London and there was a terrifying sight before us; London appeared to be all ablaze. It was indeed a well-chosen target from the German point of view. There was an obvious guide line in the river for the raid was in daylight. As we watched from the bus, we could see that the wharves on both sides of the river were ablaze. We did see one plane brought down; the pilot having bailed out. The thing was that they had so many vital targets within easy reach. There were the docks of some 250 acres, the battery of guns immediately opposite in the park (which a brother's and our own garden backed on to), and the South Bermondsey railway station and London Bridge Station plus several large factories, Peek Frean's and Shuttleworth's naming but two – all within easy striking distance. Referring back to the docks, while at that time they were crowded with ships and with timber stored in sheds and much also out in the open, it was recorded that there was half a million tons of it all ablaze with flames leaping hundreds of feet.

The bus upon which we were travelling was stopped well away from the docks. Alighting, we made our way to Hawkstone Road, leading to Abbeyfield Road, our home address. As we stood at the top of the former, across the main road just a few hundred yards away was a ship burning fiercely. Attempting to proceed home, we were stopped by the police telling us we could not proceed any further. They said that there was a delayed-action bomb behind the houses. Pointing out the situation, I was allowed to go at my own risk, leaving wife and daughter in his care. Arriving at 111 Abbeyfield Road, I got together some night-clothes, a bicycle and the mission keys. Before proceeding there, since my parents and a brother lived at the other end of Lower Road, almost opposite the entrance to Rotherhithe Tunnel, which came within the area under attack, we made our way to ascertain how they had fared. Not being able to go down the main road, which would have been a five-minute walk, and not being able to enter the park, we had about 1 mile to walk.

Getting near the tunnel we were again stopped. Explaining that I was enquiring about my parents, it made no difference: I could not go and was refused information as to the casualties. Since it was possible to see that houses opposite were destroyed, I could only assume that if they had escaped, they would surely have made their way to the mission for shelter. While busy making these enquiries, there was a lull in the bombing. They had been at it for much of the afternoon but they had not finished and it was now around 6 p.m. The guns in the park had opened up and with the planes again overhead, and because of the falling shrapnel, we decided to go down into the shelter provided by the council just inside the park gates off Union Road (now part of Jamaica Road). Going down the steep flight of steps, we could see that it was packed with people. We did not wait to see if there was any ventilation so bad was it; we decided to take our chance rather than suffocate. Keeping as near to the houses and shops as possible, we had made

War savings. In 1943 money was raised in Bermondsey to buy no fewer than twenty Flying Fortresses for the war effort. The photograph above shows a plaque commemorating the fundraising being presented to the Mayor, Cllr Albert Charles Starr, at Aylwin School in Southwark Park Road on 20 November 1943. Bermondsey's Local War Savings Committee ran a Wings for Victory Week Campaign from 6–13 March 1943 with the target of raising £800,000. The Mayor asked the Air Training Corps to select the type of aircraft; Flying Fortresses (or B-17s) were chosen because they were bombers. Lord Sherwood, the Under-Secretary of State for Air, and Major-General Eaker, a senior American airman, attended the campaign's opening ceremony in the grounds of Aylwin School. In the event, the sum of £845,113 was raised, comfortably exceeding the target. If it is thought strange that all this money was raised for American bombers, it should be added that there had also been a successful Spitfire Fund. Between September 1939 and August 1945 the stupendous sum of £7,890,000 was raised for the war effort in Bermondsey.

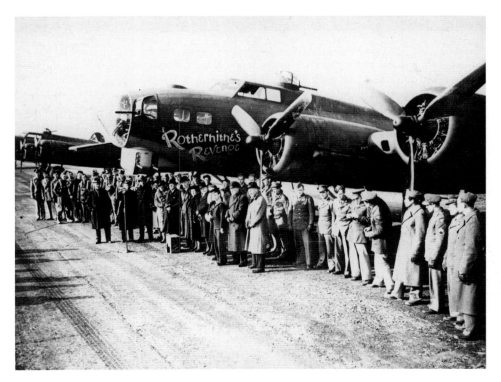

our way as far as Drummond Road. The planes being overhead and there being no shelter of any sort we laid down against the blank wall at the end of that road. Within a few minutes a bomb landed on Keeton's Road School, about three minutes' walk from where we were.

Later, there was a cessation on the part of the guns, we made our way with the hope that on arrival our fears about our family members would be cleared up, but it was not to be; the premises were securely locked. Realising it meant it had to wait for morning, we opened up and made for the semi-basement, where our daughter's first remark was 'We're safe now, Mum, aren't we?' Anxiety concerning parents meant an early trip the next morning to the tunnel for news. The house and the shop next door (my brother's) were standing but severely damaged and empty, and unable to obtain any news, I decided to phone a brother living at Egham in Surrey; there we found the answer. The brother living there was paying a visit so at the time of the bombing there were two cars outside the door. While the bombs were falling, they took shelter under the stairs and as soon as there was a lull, they went out to the cars to find them badly damaged but to their great relief they found that the engines worked and the wheels still went round and off they went to Egham.

Giving water to a publican

On another occasion, bombs demolished Parkers Row and burst the water mains until water was seeping up through the road outside leaving homes without water. I went to our basement to see how we stood, and found we could get water from the tap. I never did find out why we were so privileged. Remembering we were below water level, I secured a stand-pipe, erected it outside, and sure enough water rushed out. It did not take long for the news to travel and people came around with utensils of all kinds. Even the publican round the corner came with his bucket. I told him it was free.

Opposite page: Rotherhithe's Revenge. This is the ceremony when Cllr Albert Starr, Mayor of Bermondsey, gave the name *Rotherhithe's Revenge* to one of the Flying Fortresses. The *PLA Monthly*, the magazine of the Port of London, reported in April 1944, that this particular aircraft had been added to three others at a U.S. Eighth Army Air Force Bomber station. The other three were named *Bermondsey Battler, London Avenger* and *Bermondsey Special.* The four were known at that time as the Bermondsey War Loan fleet of American bombers. In June 1943 these aircraft were based at Ridgewell in Essex, which may well be where this picture was taken.

BERMONDSEY

ALL AID APPEAL FOR

RUSSIA

October 29th *to* November 16th
1941

SOUVENIR PROGRAMME
PRICE 3d.

Above: A National Savings rally in Abbey Street in 1945. The speaker is Ben Smith, a Member of Parliament for Rotherhithe.

Left: Help to Russia in 1941. One of the best-known British operations in the Second World War was the running of the Arctic convoys to Murmansk to take military supplies to Stalin's Russia. In Bermondsey too, aid to Russia was a regular part of the wartime agenda. Here we have the cover of an extensive programme of events run from 29 October to 16 November 1941, just a few months after Hitler's forces invaded Russia. It included a grand civic parade on 9 November, going from Spa Road to Southwark Park and featuring military units, the Civil Defence and voluntary bodies. A year later, Bermondsey Borough Council reported that an Aid to Russia Week in Bermondsey had raised £1,769 10s 9d. The Russian Ambassador, Ivan Maisky, referred to it as a 'splendid sum'. Mrs Churchill headed the national organisation, which arranged regular flag days. In one list of ten such days for different purposes, Mrs Churchill's Aid to Russia Day yielded the second highest collection. The firm C.W. Martin & Sons, of the Alaska Factory in Grange Road, produced no fewer than 137,000 garments for Mrs Churchill's Aid to Russia Fund during the war.

Bermondsey water cart on active service. Some of Bermondsey Borough Council's water carts were requisitioned in 1944 in connection with the campaign in Normandy and beyond, for dust on airfields was a serious problem and a prodigious quantity of water was needed to tackle it. They were assigned to the Royal Engineers and were used to water airfields, firstly in France and later in Belgium and the Netherlands. Two carts were attached to the 78th Road Construction Co., 16th Airfield Construction Group, Royal Engineers. The 'flash' seen attached to this picture was sent to Bermondsey council by the officers and men of the 78th Co., together with an account of the carts' record. The carts, it is recorded, 'at last succumbed to the rigours of the campaign at a point 30 miles north of Eindhoven'. Their last resting-place was the airfield at Volkel. The carts had been built in the wheelwrights' shop in the Neckinger Depot in Bermondsey. On one occasion the 78th Road Construction Co. was sent ahead of some tanks to clear the town of Argentan and so to let the tanks through. The water-carts went as well. When the carts passed the tanks, an irate brigadier halted the convoy and demanded to know who was in command of 'this bloody circus'. Written authority was at once produced, and the brigadier was forced to watch his mighty tanks preceded into battle by a pair of Bermondsey water-carts.

A Bermondsey Childhood

By Barbara Stamford-Plows

Dunton Road in the war

Grandad Plows used to sit in the garden watching the signals. Railwaymen along the line would signal when enemy planes were over Kent, so we had an early warning before the siren went, but they didn't always get as far as London. I don't remember being frightened by the air raids; I was too young to understand and was a placid child anyway. My brother Victor was entirely different. He was two-and-a-half years younger than me and the war had been going on for some time so my mother was nervous which must have affected him. I remember sleeping in the double bed with my mother, with Vic in a cot alongside. As soon as the warning siren woke us, Vic would be standing up in his cot screaming. Mum kept all her papers and valuables in a handbag by the bed; she would grab the bag and Vic and head for the shelter. I would grab my pink teddy and my bag and follow her. One day, after a daylight raid, I came out of the shelter and found a dead butterfly – I was convinced that the bombs had got it! Another wartime memory is of sitting on a potty in the middle of dust and rubble and with the window-frame leaning against the wall. This was at my maternal grandmother's after they'd caught the blast of a bomb dropping nearby. I still remember the bloodcurdling sound of an air-raid warning. Years later, when I was a student nurse at Epping, I heard it again and automatically stood still and looked up, but it was only a local signal to call out the fire brigade!

Nursery school in the war

Vic and I went to nursery school at Kintore Way next to the Boutcher School, so that our mother could go out to work. It was the summer before my third birthday so I don't remember a lot about it. We sometimes had to go into the big shelter in the playground so there must have been some daylight raids. After lunch every day we slept on canvas camp-beds in the playground – I had a problem with putting on my shoes, I couldn't tell left from right. My mother marked the insides L and R but that was not much help because I couldn't always remember which foot was which either! We didn't stay at nursery for very long as Vic screamed continually and never settled down. He was a very nervous baby and my mother had to take him to see a child psychologist – at the age of eighteen months! – who said that he was 'one of Hitler's casualties'.

VE Night

I was nearly five when the war ended. I remember VE night – every house had open doors and windows and all the lights were blazing. The grown-ups had all gone mad, my grandmother's piano was out in the street, my mother playing it, and everyone was dancing. My big cousin Vera took me round the streets to see the bonfires – they were on every bomb-site and in every street. I was eventually put to bed but I could hear the singing and laughing until I went to sleep.

Parkers Row and Dockhead after a V2 attack in March 1945. A V2 landed in Parkers Row in the evening of 3 March 1945 opposite the Roman Catholic church. Buildings near the explosion were demolished and those for up to 500 yards around suffered severe blast damage. The whole of nearby Oxley Street, a small backstreet, was destroyed. The church and the priests' house adjoining were very close to the blast. Three priests were killed but a fourth was rescued after a protracted operation in which one rescuer, Edward Heming, worked head downwards in perilous conditions. The priest, although badly injured, survived. His rescuer was afterwards awarded the George Cross.

Following pages: A victory party in Long Lane in 1945. It was held outside the Ship public house, towards the Bermondsey Street end. The building still stands but is no longer a pub. The tradition of parties for children in the street began with Coronations and Jubilees earlier in the twentieth century and was widely observed on VE Day.

Other local titles published by The History Press

Southwark Remembered
JOHN D. BEASLEY

This fascinating compilation was put together from a series of illustrated local history articles written by John Beasley for the *South London Press* since 1997. It contains over 100 photographs, reminiscences and stories from this historic area of South London and will appeal to all who grew up or have lived there.

7524 2241 3

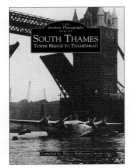

South Thames: Tower Bridge to Thamesmead
HILARY HEFFERNAN

This book is a collection of old photographs that record activities on and around London's river as seen from its south side. Rivermen recall times not far distant when there was sometimes so much river traffic that it was possible to walk across decks from one side to the other! Long gone scenes and long lost characters reappear in these pages that will delight all who have had any association with this great waterway.

7524 0670 1

The Annual Hop: London to Kent
HILARY HEFFERNAN

Using over 200 old photographs and a host of nostalgic anecdotes from the hop-pickers themselves the author has compiled a fascinating record of this annual event that involved so many Londoners and their families. Partly as a holiday from the smoke and partly as a source of extra income thousands migrated each year to the hopfields of Kent to pick hops. These are their stories and photographs.

7524 0379 6

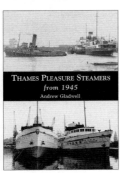

Thames Pleasure Steamers from 1945
ANDREW GLADWELL

For a generation of Londoners a trip to the seaside aboard one of the many paddle steamers was a traditional and essential part of summer. Many of the early boats went to Dunkirk and never returned. By the end of the 1940s the stage was set for a new 'Golden Age' of the pleasure steamer and a new and grander breed of boat began to appear. This book charts this period with over 200 old photographs.

7524 3085 8

If you are interested in purchasing other books published by The History Press, or in case you have difficulty finding any of our books in your local bookshop, you can also place orders directly through our website
www.thehistorypress.co.uk